THE STORY IN STONE

A CHRONICLE OF THE KENSINGTON STONE

BY

JAN BERNARD STOLZ

THE STORY IN STONE

First published in April 2018 by CreateSpace.com

OTHER BOOKS
BY
JAN BERNARD STOLZ

The Men Who Made the Comics
My Place among the Microbes
"THE LOST DUTCHMAN" JACOB WALTZ
The Song of the Poor Clares
THE SAGA OF SNOWSHOE THOMPSON

You can contact Jan by email at:
Stolz_jan@yahoo.com

THE KENSINGTON STONE

"Whenever I was asked about the Kensington Rune Stone, the question was always *"Is it real?"* The answer was, *"Absolutely! Columbus was too late!"*

Darwin Ohman

THE STORY IN STONE

TABLE OF CONTENTS

CHAPTER 1

THE DISCOVERY

"A new discovery has revealed that the Vikings may have travelled hundreds of miles further into North America than previously thought. It's well known that they reached the tip of the continent more than 1,000 years ago, but the full extent of their exploration has remained a mystery."[1]

Only since the second half of the 20th Century have historians and scholars realized that their assessment of world history, especially when it came to the European "discovery" of the Americas, was all wrong. Although the Icelandic sagas had told the story of its discovery by Vikings as early as 985, they were largely discounted as fiction – that is until 1960 when Leif Erikson's home, Leifsbudir, was uncovered at L'Anse aux Meadows in present-day Newfoundland.

Suddenly, Columbus was a Johnny-come-lately, his title as America's discoverer quietly stripped and his place in the history books drastically reduced from an entire chapter to but a couple of paragraphs. For the truth was, the Nordic peoples had been making regular journeys back and forth to the New World, harvesting timber from the virgin forests; grapes (and grape vines); even wild turkeys (not to mention anything else they could make money on) since about the year 1000.

The written versions of the orally recited centuries-old sagas of the Viking were set down on paper around 1220, and also included the journeys to, and exploits in, the North American continent which are encompassed in two accounts: *The Saga of Erik the Red* and *The Saga of the Greenlanders*, (both of which are reproduced in full in the final chapter of this book.)

Not only did they know all about the continent; they were well aware of its inhabitants, which, it turns out, were the main reason why the Norsemen didn't (or couldn't) colonize the "new" country, as they had with Iceland and Greenland.

---

[1] Dan Snow – Today's Magazine, April 1, 2016

Great Britain first felt the ferocity of a Viking raid in 793 AD when, sailing out of 'viks'[2] in Norway, they rowed their ships onto the beach at Lindisfarne and attacked the wealthy monastery there which was quickly overrun. Those who attempted to put up a defense were promptly slaughtered; all survivors were taken prisoners to be sold as slaves. The Vikings looted the monastery of anything and everything of value then quickly departed, rowing away. This proved so successful a tactic that an identical attack on the monastery at Portmahomack, on the eastern coast of England, was quick to follow. These incidents are commonly regarded as the beginning of the Viking era, as historians refer to the time period ranging from 793 to 1100.

Our best description of the Norse raiders comes from the Arab chronicler Ibn Fadlan, a represenitive of the Abbasid Caliph of Baghdad, who, in 921, met Rus[3] traders of Swedish origin near the Middle Volga. Impressed by their appearance he described them as *"perfect physical specimens, tall as date palms, blonde and ruddy."* He noted Viking women maintained important roles in their society, especially compared to other cultures at the time. For instance a woman not only had complete authority over the farm when her husband was away, she could own land and had the right to demand a divorce if she no longer wanted to be married.

Fadlan describes the women, saying *"each one wears on either breast a box of iron, silver, copper or gold; the value of the box indicates the wealth of the husband. Each box has a ring from which depends a knife. The women wear neck rings of gold and silver, one for each 10,000 dirhems which her husband is worth; some women have many."*

According to his account, the Rus warriors would pray to their gods *"I would like you to do me the favor of sending me a merchant who has large quantities of dinars and dirhams and who will buy everything I want and not argue with me over the price."*

Impressed as he was, Fadlan was disgusted by their overall lack of hygiene as well as their uninhibited sexual practices. *"They are the filthiest of God's creatures. They have no modesty in defecation and urination, nor do they wash after pollution from orgasm, nor do they wash their hands after eating. With them are pretty slave girls destined for sale to merchants: a man will have sexual intercourse with his slave girl while his companion looks on. Sometimes whole groups will come together in this fashion, each in the presence of others. A merchant who arrives to buy a slave girl from them may have to wait and look on while a Rus completes the act of intercourse with a slave girl."*

Such were the men who took part in the hit-and–run raids, like those on Lindisfarne and Portmahomack, surprise attacks which usually took place during the summer to take advantage of the more favorable weather. All were typically prearranged at mass

---

[2] Vik is the Gallic word for bay or inlet; hence the term vik-ing or Viking.
[3] The Arab term for Goth

assemblies held during the winter, with usually one person organizing the entire affair. It was his responsibility to arranged for the necessary ships, both Drakkars and Knöörrs[4], and to recruit the number of men needed, each of whom was required to swear loyalty and complete obedience to the leader. Thus, voyages could be organized by *any* Viking, provided he could bring together the required ships, supplies, and men. Upon returning, the loot was divided, half for the organizer, half for the crew. (It was the Noblemen, usually acting on their king's orders that mounted the enormous raids, such as the Danish expedition into Spain in 968 in which Jarl Gundraed commanded 100 ships carrying 8000 men.)

By the 9th century Norwegian *Norse* (or *Northmen*) dominated most of northern England, Scotland and Ireland (founding Dublin, which, along with York, became important Viking trade centers) while the southern English coasts were constantly harassed by the *Goth* (Swedes). The Viking culture quickly expanded into areas surrounding the Scandinavian states, while at the same time they invaded Orkney, Shetland, Fair Isle, conquered Normandy in France, parts of Italy and the Levant, even making contact with regions as far away as the Caspian Sea in the east; not to mention their expansion westward into Iceland, Greenland, and Newfoundland (which they called Vinland) as they island-hopped across the North Atlantic.

ON TO VINLAND

It is only fitting that the discovery of the "new World" came about because of the two most dangerous (and sadly, most typical) of human emotions – stubbornness and pride. A Viking was not one to turn the other cheek when challenged or affronted and the resulting bloody duels often reverberated far beyond their homeland. And no reverberation was felt as much as that from Erik Thorvaldson, known to history as "Erik the Red".

Erik's children were: Leif, Thorvald, Thorstein, and Freydis, his step-daughter. Around the year 980 Erik was charged with murdering of two fellow Vikings and was first forced to relocate to Iceland's west coast, then finally banished from the island altogether. *"Erik said to his people that he purposed to seek for the land which Gunnbjorn, the son of Ulf the Crow, saw when he was driven westwards over the ocean, and discovered Gunnbjarnarsker (Gunnbjorn's rock). He promised that he would return to visit his friends if he found the land."*[5]

Erik described endless rolling green pastures, perfect for raising cattle, as well as an abundance of fish, whales and seals. Hundreds of fellow Vikings went back with him and settled there. Meanwhile, Erik's son, Leif had *"joined the body-guard of King Olaf Tryggvason, and the king formed an excellent opinion of him."*

---

[4] Also Knorr or Knarr - a type of cargo ship
[5] Chapter 2 from The Saga of Erik the Red

The king asked Leif to spread Christianity to Greenland and Leif agreed and in the year 998 Leif outfitted a Knorr.

"Leif set sail as soon as he was ready. He was tossed about a long time out at sea, and lighted upon lands of which before he had no expectation. There were fields of wild wheat, and the vine-tree in full growth. There were also the trees which were called maples; and they gathered of all this certain tokens; some trunks so large that they were used in house-building. Leif came upon men who had been shipwrecked, and took them home with him, and gave them sustenance during the winter. Thus did he show his great munificence and his graciousness when he brought Christianity to the land, and saved the shipwrecked crew. He was called Leif the Lucky."

As best as can be determined, Leif sailed up Greenland's west coast, traversed the Davis Strait then turned south past Baffin Island before coming to Newfoundland.

"They were out at sea two half-days. Then they came to land, and rowed along it in boats, and explored it, and found there flat stones, many and so great that two men might well lie on them stretched on their backs with heel to heel. Polar-foxes were there in abundance. This land they gave name to, and called it Helluland (stone-land)."[6]

"Then they sailed with northerly winds two half-days, and there was then land before them, and on it a great forest and many wild beasts. An island lay in the south-east off the land, and they found bears thereon, and called the island Bjarney (Bear Island); but the mainland, where the forest was, they called Markland (forest-land).

Leif disembarked in Vinland[7] building a settlement he named Leifsbudir consisting of a long-house and a three other structures. According to the Sagas this land was fertile, had good weather and plenty of wildlife; its rivers and lakes teeming with salmon and other species of fish.

Leif and his men spent three years in the new land, gathering timber, grapes and grape vines, as well as a few wild turkeys before returning home to Bratthalid with their ship fully laden with timber, a scarce and valuable commodity in Greenland. It was proof positive of his find and was very well received. The following year his father, Erik the Red, died leaving Leif to take over the administration of the farm, thus Leif was never able to return to Vinland.

The follow-up expedition was led by Leif's brother Thorvald in 1001. As per agreement, Thorvald was allowed the use of the buildings at Leifsbudir. His party first made what repairs were necessary and expanded the dwellings, then spent the next two years exploring the coasts of Vinland. On one occasion they stumbled upon natives, (in this instance, the Thule, ancestors of today's Inuit) which the Vikings referred to as the Skrælingar (*"wretched people".*)[8]

---

[6] The Saga of Erik the Red – Chapter 8
[7] I use 'Vinland' here as a general term for the Americas
[8] I have also seen it translated as "barbarian" "foreigner" "weak" "sickly" "false friend" and "skin wearer"

The North Americans and the North Europeans had known and had contact with each other ever since Erik had established Greenland, and both being of similar mind and temperament, violence was the usual interaction between the two. In Vinland it proved to be no different with the Thule attacking Thorvald's ships almost the moment the made land. Although the Vikings fought them off, Thorvald was mortally wounded in the fray.

"I have been wounded under my arm." A contemporary account recorded Thorvald as saying. *"An arrow flew between the edge of the ship and the shield into my armpit. Here is the arrow, and this wound will cause my death."*

(Indeed, archaeologists have since discovered arrowheads in the remains of several buried Norse explorers.) This would render Thorvald the distinction of being the first modern European to be buried in America; it also forced his party to return to Greenland early, but even so, fully laden with timber and grapes.

A third expedition to Vinland was then organized by the youngest brother, Thorstein. Sadly, his ship was thrown off course by a storm and all on board, except for a woman, were lost at sea.

I 1004, a wealthy merchant named Thorfinn Karlsefni, on a trading voyage to Greenland, met and married Gudrid Thorbjarnardottir, Thorvald's beautiful and charismatic widow. (A history of Iceland written in 1120, as well as church records, back-up the genealogies and dates in the sagas.)

During that winter at Brattahlid *"much playing at backgammon and telling of stories went on"* Leif regaled Thorfinn with the wonders of Vinland. Immediately enthralled with the immense wealth the natural resources offered, Thorfinn began plotting his own journey to the new country. Yet, *Erik the Red's saga* makes the planning sound somewhat haphazard, noting that various other Norse chiefs decided to join the expedition seemingly on the spur of the moment.

In the spring of 1005, seven years after Leif's initial voyage, Thorfinn and Gudrid set off from the west coast of Greenland with three ships and a band of Norse following Leif Erikson's original route.

Traveling in two ships, Thorfinn's party of 160 (which included whole families) sought to established a colony at Leifsbudir at first using the same dwellings Leif and Thorvald had constructed, which he renamed Straumfjord (stream fiord - where Thorfinn's son Snorri was born) and remained for three years. Thorfinn also established a second site 400 miles further south he named Hóp (lagoon).

It's been a long-held theory by scholars that Thorfinn was the principal teller of the sagas (which would explain why he plays such a major role in them) and for years the sagas challenged scholars to match the place names mentioned in them to real topography.

What is known is that during the three years in Vinland Thorfinn's party faced a constant threat of attack by the native Thule warriors. On one occasion the Vikings were approached by the Thule offering to exchange furs for weapons. Karlsefni, suspicious of their motives forbid his men from trading weapons or armor no matter what was offered in trade and some problems between the two groups resulted.

It seemed that even the smallest provocation could touch off a battle, such as when a  bull escaped from the Norse camp, terrifying the native warriors who then attacked the settlement at Straumfjord, where two Vikings were killed in the resulting skirmish.

Unlike their counterparts 500 years later, the Vikings weren't curious about nor surprised by the native people. In fact, the Norse and the Skrælingar[9] (in this case the Thule) had come into contact with each other on a fairly regular basis ever since Erik the Red settled Greenland.

Located northwest of Greenland the island of Thule (called Qaanaaq today) is part of the Kingdom of Denmark; the Thule people of the 11th century being the direct biological ancestors of the modern Inuit, and had come into regular contact with the Viking almost from the moment Erik the Red set foot on Greenland's shore. They were commonly referred to as both their tribal name, Thule, and the more general term used for any Native American, Skrælingar. But, for whatever reason, the two groups just could not, or would not, get along.

"Now, when they sailed from Vinland, they had a southern wind, and reached Markland, and found five Skrælingar; one was a bearded man, two were women, two children. Karlsefni's people caught the children, but the others escaped and sunk down into the earth. And they took the children with them, and taught them their speech, and they were baptized."[10]

The validity of the statement above (that two Native American children were caught) was verified in recent findings in mitochondrial DNA research, DNA that is passed only from mother to child. Scientists have found more than 80 living Icelanders with a genetic variation similar to one found mostly in Native Americans. This signature DNA entered Icelandic bloodlines around the time period of 1000 AD (which closely corresponds to the sagas) when the first Viking-American Indian child was probably born.

In fact, it is most likely because of this kidnapping that Thorfinn, along with his family and surviving crew were finally *forced* to abandon their settlement around the year 1008. (Thorfinn and Gudrid eventually resettled in Iceland, Thorfinn's childhood home.)

---

[9] Skrælingar was the generic Icelandic term for any Native American
[10] The Saga of Erik the Red – Chapter 14

The fifth and last documented voyage to Vinland was organized by Leif's step-sister, Freydis Eiriksdaughter (Eiríksdóttir) and her husband Thorvard (Þorvarðr)[11] who lived in Garde. Freydis was in a class of her own; very haughty and not well liked she married the narrow-minded Thorvard chiefly because of his money. The two of them made this 5th expedition to the new world in partnership with two Icelandic merchants, brothers Helgi and Finnbogi which resulted in betrayal and savage murder – all instigated by Freydis!

Reading "The Saga of Erik the Red"[12] it appears the separate voyages of Thorfinn Karlsefni and Freydis Eiriksdaughter have been combined into a singular event. (Another reason to believe this saga originated with Karlsefni.)

It's with the story of Freydis the sagas of discovery end, the subsequent utilitarian visits (mostly for timber, but also for foodstuffs such as grapes and even turkeys) to Vinland, Markland and the other lands for the next 350 years, not considered worthy of being recorded.

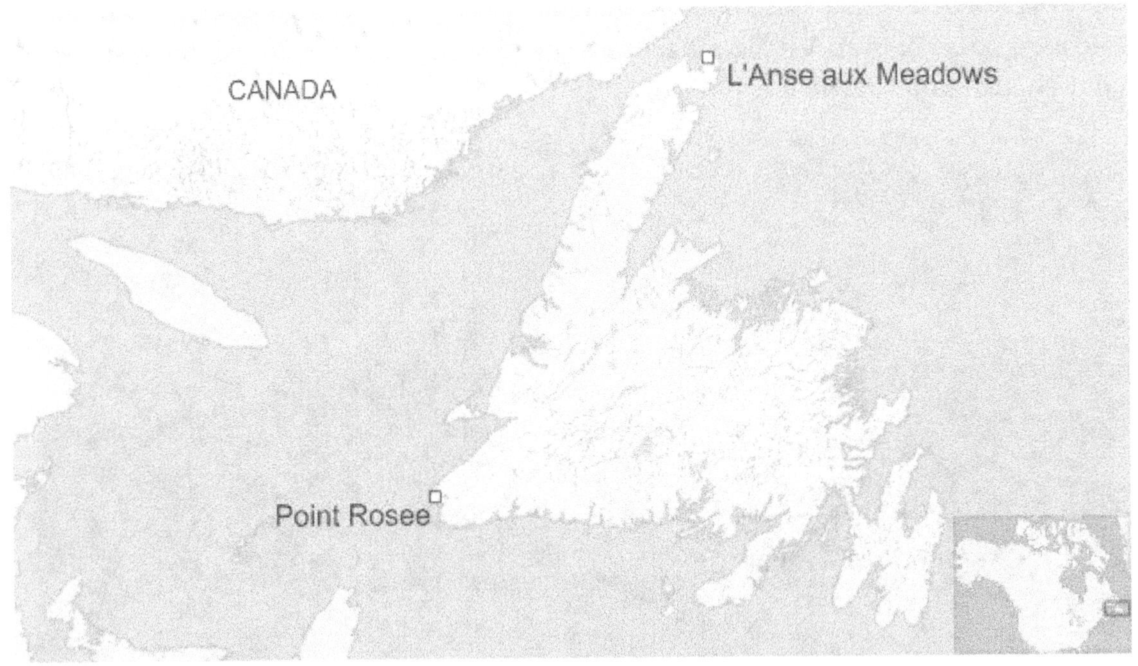

Up until the mid-20th century few serious historians gave much credence to the sagas, believing a Viking trip to the New World centuries before Columbus was preposterous. Besides, where was the proof?

Then, in 1960, at L'Anse aux Meadows on the very northernmost tip of Newfoundland, explorer Helge Ingstad and his wife, Anne Stine Ingstad, an archaeologist, discovered the remains of eight long houses proven to be of Nordic design. The structures were dated to the year 1000, closely corresponding to the journeys in the sagas. Typical Viking objects were also found, such as pins, stone lamps, and some

---

[11] It is not known who Thorvard's father was, hence there is no patronymic for him
[12] See Chapter 7

carved wooden pieces believed to be ship fittings. Leifsbudir/Straumfjord had been discovered at long last.

Further excavations from 1973 to 1976 uncovered even more utensils and over 2000 pieces of worked wood; mostly debris from smoothing and trimming the timber that was shipped to Greenland. In 1978 the Canadian Government reconstructed the long-house and two other buildings, and declared the location a UNESCO World Heritage Site.

The sagas, however, mention another homesteading site, Hóp. But search as they may, no archeological proof of this second site could be found - until 2016, that is, when Sarah Parcak and her team, using satellite imagery, discovered some anomalies at several sites in Newfoundland that appeared worth following up. They eventually focused their efforts on the headland called Point Rosee at the very western tip of Newfoundland, 400 miles further south from L'Anse aux Meadows. The site overlooked two bays or lagoons, offering protection for ships from any wind direction and Parcak noticed oddities in the soil that stood out; patterns and discolorations that suggested artificial, man-made structures, possibly even Viking longhouses. Field work soon confirmed her suspicions and the outlines of a longhouse 100 feet by 25 1/2 feet were uncovered.

The Sagas were finally vindicated; Leif Eriksson *had* landed in the New World – in Newfoundland! His prized Leifsbudir being located at L'Anse aux Meadows, and the later homestead, Hóp, at Point Rosee. There is now ample archeological evidence at both sites to prove the Vikings did indeed visit the North American continent around the year 1000, centuries before any other Europeans. The Icelandic sagas were proven to relate actual events, not "fairy stories."

But the question remains – why didn't they establish permanent residence in the new world just as they had in Great Britain, Iceland and Greenland?

As early as 850AD the Vikings *"were able to penetrate deep into England, making their way along the rivers and ancient Roman roads, setting up overwintering camps, and wreaking havoc on the Anglo Saxons. "It seems the Vikings are after something a little bit different at this stage."* Jane Kershaw, from the University of Oxford, said. *"They're still after portable wealth, but they start to have an eye toward acquiring land as well. They start to see England as somewhere they might be able to settle and reestablish themselves as lords with their own families."*[13]

One would think that in the unexploited utopia of natural resources the Americas offered, Viking colonization of the areas would have been a natural progression after its discovery; and indeed, Thorfinn's party of 160 which included whole families in 1005 seemed to be just that. So what happened? Why didn't they stay?

As reported in Smithsonian Magazine, *"more and more scholars focus on climate change as the reason the Vikings couldn.t make a go of it in the New World. The scholars suggest that the western Atlantic suddenly turned too cold even for Vikings. The great sailing trips of Leif and Thorfinn took place in the first half of the 11th century, during a climatic period in the North Atlantic called the Medieval Warming, a time of long, warm summers and scarce sea ice. Beginning in the 12th century, however, the weather started to deteriorate with the first frissons of what scholars call the Little Ice Age."*

But the rugged Norsemen were used to the brutal winters of the north Atlantic – they wouldn't let a little thing like the weather, no matter how cold it got, stand in the way of immense wealth just sitting there, waiting to be taken advantage of. And from all indications, it didn't. Voyages to the New World to extract timber became more or less regular ventures, albeit hazardous. (Who knows how many Viking vessels lay at the bottom of the North Atlantic seas.)

No, the real reason the Vikings didn't stay in the New World is laid out clearly in the sagas; it was because the people who had inhabited the lands for at least 15,000 years prior to the Norsemen's appearance didn't want these intruders making a home there.

At first, the Vikings engaged in peaceful interaction, even trade, with Native Americans. But it never seem to last. *"Despite everything the land had to offer there, they were under constant threat of attack from its prior inhabitants."* One Norsemen recorded.

Relations with Indians, no matter which tribe, always deteriorated from bad to worse until in the end the two factions were at constant war with one another and peaceful contact between the two became out of the question.

Maybe colonization was out of the question, but the New World still offered immense wealth in natural resources; a man could become rich by just harvesting timber (a rare and valuable commodity on Greenland)–and it was free for the taking! The potential rewards were well worth dodging a few spears and arrows. And if all this was on the coastline of the vast new country – what potential treasures lay within?

---

[13] "The Viking Great Army" by Daniel Weiss – from Archaeology Magazine, March/April 2018 – pg. 51

It *had* to be a question the Vikings asked themselves. But if there ever *were* any Viking expeditions into the heart of what would become the United States, could they have left any evidence of their voyage behind?

CHAPTER 2

THE STORY IN STONE

Minnesota was still a wilderness in the 1830s when the first European hunters and trappers began to traverse the future state on their way to points further west. It wasn't until the 1850s when the first Swedish immigrants homesteaded and began building farms there.

The tilling of the lands in the area eventually known as Kensington came about 1870; a landscape consisting mostly of islands of stony glacial deposits, many covered with stunted timber and many still surrounded by marshes. The area was difficult to farm, and at first was simply used as the community woodlot. It wasn't until 1886 that a railroad was built through the district and its station, called Kensington, was established, giving the area its present day name. With this new ease of access the less desirable lands in the area finally began to be homesteaded.

One of these newcomers was Swedish immigrant Olof Ohman, along with his wife Karin, and two sons, Edward and Art, who settled in the area in 1891 and began hacking a life out of the wilderness. Life was hard but good to the Ohman's as over the years they established a good relationship and respected place within the community.

On a warm summer day in 1898 Olof and 10 year-old Edward set out to clear a couple of trees from a hill on the south-west corner of his land; their story best being told in Olof's own words:

"I, Olof Ohman, of the town of Solem, Douglas County, state of Minnesota, being duly sworn, make the following statement:[14]

"I am 54 years of age, and was born in Helsingland, Sweden, from where I emigrated [sic] to America in the year 1881, and settled upon my farm in Section 14, Township of Solem, in 1891.

---

[14] From Olof Ohman's affidavit (July 20, 1909); first printed in The Journal of American History, IV, 178 (1910)

"In the month of August, 1898, while accompanied by my son Edward, I was engaged in grubbing upon a timbered elevation, surrounded by marshes, in the southern corner of my land, about 500 feet west of my neighbor's, Nils Flaaten's house, and in full view thereof."

"Upon removing an asp[15], measuring about 10 inches in diameter at the base, I discovered a flat stone inscribed with characters, to me unintelligible. The stone lay just beneath the surface of the ground in a slightly slanting position, with the corner almost protruding. The 2 largest roots of the tree clasped the stone in such a manner that the stone must have been there at least as long as the tree.

"One of the roots penetrated directly downward and was flat on the side next to the stone. The other root extended almost horizontally across the stone and made at its edge a right angled turn downward. This root was almost 3 inches in diameter."

When Olof first glimpsed the stone, the inscription was hidden, buried face-down, making the object appear to be just a large square chunk of rock the tree's roots had overgrown and which now anchored it into the soil. Frustrated by this stony barrier Olof found he couldn't cut the roots away with his axe without damaging the blade so he began digging out the soil from around the slab of rock until he was able to work a hoe down alongside the stone to judge its thickness. He was pleased when he was able to hook the hoe underneath it, then, after considerable digging and prying he managed to flip the tree stump over, the rock still held tightly in the grasp of its roots.

As Olof took a much deserved break, young Willie Sarsland, a neighbor of the Ohmans and friend of Edward, walked up to see what they were doing. Edward pointed out the stone clutched in the roots of the tree – then noticed something more amidst the caked on dirt; something that looked like - writing. Intrigued, Edward dusted the face of the stone with his cloth cap then called the inscription to his father's attention. Olof stepped over to take a look and was immediately fascinated. He cut the stone free of the tree's roots then used their bucket of drinking water to wash off the dirt.

"Upon washing off the surface dirt, the inscription presented a weathered appearance which to me appeared just as old as the untouched parts of the stone. I immediately called my neighbor, Nils Flaaten's attention to the discovery and he came over the same afternoon and inspected the stone and the stump under which it was found."

Mr. Flaaten:

"I, Nils Flaten, of the town of Solem, Douglas County, Minnesota, being duly sworn, make the following statement:[16]

"I am 65 years of age, and was born in Tinn, Telemarken, Norway, and settled at my present home in the town of Solem in 1884. One day in August, 1898, my neighbor, Olof Ohman, who was engaged in grubbing timber about 500 feet west of my house, and in full

---

[15] Aspen tree (populos tremuloides)
[16] From Nils Flaten's affidavit (July 20, 1909)

view of same, came to me and told me he had discovered a stone inscribed with ancient characters. I accompanied him to the alleged place of discovery and saw a stone about 30 inches long, 16 inches wide, and 6 inches thick, which was covered with strange characters upon 2 sides and for more than half their length. The inscription presented a very ancient and weathered appearance.

"Mr. Ohman showed me an asp tree about 8 inches to 10 inches in diameter at its base, beneath which he alleged the stone was found. The two largest roots of the asp were flattened on their inner surface and bent by nature in such a way as to exactly conform to the outlines of the stone.

"I inspected the hole and can testify to the fact that the stone had been there prior to the growth of the tree, as the spot was in close proximity to my house. I had visited the same spot earlier in the day before Mr. Ohman had cut down the tree and also many times previously - but I had never seen anything suspicious there. Besides the asp, the roots of which embraced the stone, the spot was also covered by a very heavy growth of underbrush."

This photograph was taken at the find site in 1910. Shown, from left to right, are Edwin Bjerklund, Nils Flaaten (with marker) and Olof Ohman.
(Nils' farm can be seen on the far right.)

The runes were legible but even after washing tightly packed with dried mud. Olof first attempted to gouge out the caked-in earth with a wooden stick, which just broke, then making an error in judgment he would come to regret, he scraped out the carvings using an old iron nail. The resulting scratches would come to haunt the rune stone, as its detractors claimed that they were the "obvious" marks of recent carving. (However, one only has to study the stone closely to see the scratches are deep down in the runes, the remainder of the carved surfaces showing obvious weathering.)

As the news of the discovery quickly spread, people began flocking to Ohman's farm to get a look at the curious stone (a dozen of whom would later leave written statements confirming the manner of the tree stump and how the roots were flattened on one side conforming exactly to the stone.)

Then one of the visitors wondered aloud if the marks might have been carved by white or Indian robbers who had buried a treasure there. It was a statement heard by at least one other, for within an hour the entire hillside where the stone was found was under siege by dozens of men with shovels and pickaxes. Only after several days of hard digging, leaving the hill riddled with craters, did the enthusiasm over possible buried treasure finally wane.

The flattened roots were in exact conformation to the root marks on the stone, making it apparent that the stone had been buried for a long time; at the very *least* 20 to 30 years (although an aspen tree of similar size[17] (about 10 inches across the center) was later cut down and counting its rings showed it to be 72 years old). Either way, this automatically precluded a hoax by Ohman, who didn't even land in this country until 1881; unless one actually believes Olof went off into the wilderness as soon as he walked off the boat, carved the stone, planted a tree on top of it, then didn't come back for 17 years; or somehow managed to carve a blank stone in the time between uncovering it and when Nils Flaten saw it, a matter, at most, of just 15-20 minutes.[18]

Ohman's statement continues:

"I kept the stone in my possession for a few days then left it in the Bank of Kensington, where it remained for inspection for several months."

It was at the bank that one of the customers studying it happened to mention the inscription looked to him as if it was in runic characters. Olof was asked to make a rubbing of the inscription which was then sent off for evaluation to the University of Minnesota.

Here it came into the hands of one Olaus Beda, Professor of Scandinavian languages. Finding Olof's rubbing was not as sharply defined as he'd like, Beda then asked Samuel Siverts, an acquaintance of his in Kensington, to make another, more detailed tracing of the inscription and forward it to him, which he did. Copies were then sent around the country and to Sweden. (It was during this time Olof acquired a couple of books about runes and attempted to translate the inscription himself.) Breda was the very first linguist to examine the stone, studying the inscription for a couple of months before revealing a partial translation of it.

---

[17] After the stone was declared a fake Ohman saw no point in saving the original stump
[18] It was determined by professional stone carvers that it took *at least* two days (if not longer) to shape the stone and carve the inscription.

Meanwhile, excitement over the Stone continued to grow. On February 20, 1899, The Chicago Tribune reported that the stone could be *"the oldest record of American history."* This was followed up the very next day, on February 21, 1899, by The Chicago Daily Inter Ocean, which noted that *"if authentic it is destined to revolutionize previous researches of archaeologists."*

Then Professor Breda announced his findings and was quickly interviewed by local newspapers. He stated that, in *his* expert opinion, *"I don't believe the inscription is genuine, and for the following reasons: first, it talks about a mixture of Swedes and Norwegians on the same expedition, which is contrary to all accounts of the Vinland voyages"*. Second, Breda (who was totally unaware of rune numerals) declared the inscription was not Old Norse at all, but some combination of Swedish, Norwegian, and English; an impossible mixture for any 11th century expedition.

Ohman continues:

"During this interval, it was sent to Chicago for inspection and was soon returned in the same state in which it was sent."

The Stone itself was then shipped to the Germanic Department of Northwestern University where it could be personally inspected by Professor George O. Curme for authentication.

However, Professor Curme also proved skeptical. Although he did note the stone's weathering, he stated that *"I have sent to Minnesota and asked that the ground about the tree be dug up and examined. Bones can be kept intact for a longer period than 500 years if the soil is favorable and some remains ought to be found."*

Curme believed the stone was actually a grave marker and expected the bodies of the 'ten men red with blood' to be buried at the discovery site. But treasure seekers had already dug up the entire area and, along with no treasure, found no evidence of any human remains. Even so, he had a party excavate the site but nothing was turned up.

Then Professor Curme created another legend with his declaration *"The most positive proof that the inscription is not of the ancient origin claimed by its discoverers is the fact that the crevices which form the letters are of a lighter color than the outer surface of the stone; this could hardly be the case if the stone had been buried for the 600 years that must have elapsed provided the inscription is genuine."*

This lighter color, of course is in reference to the scraping Olof did with the nail to clear mud from the runes. Any careful examination would have revealed this, but instead, in a statement which almost sounds resentful, another rush to judgment created a myth that persists to this day. And note that Curme calls it the *most positive proof* of a hoax.

Also, while the stone was in Curme's possession, the first known photographs of the Kensington Rune Stone (previous page) were taken by John F. Stewart and sent to scholars in Europe. Upon being notified the smug scholars openly laughed at the idea of a pre-Columbian expedition into the very heart of America, calling it a *"fantastic absurdity which did not merit serious consideration."*

They couldn't believe these Americans were serious; a Viking expedition into Minnesota? It was sheer fantasy! After all, their very reputations were at stake and they dared not gamble them in the court of established academic opinion, which even to this day has a well-known resistance to new discoveries; especially those which challenge long held perceptions, especially when they are proven erroneous.

It was the considered opinion of these academics that such a journey as described on the Stone was not only improbable, but quite *impossible*. After only a cursive glance at the photographs they proclaimed the runic inscription a *"clumsy fraud"* probably perpetrated by some Swedish or Norwegian immigrant; and that was it. Theirs was considered the final word on the subject and the Stone, now branded a forgery, was sent back to Ohman.

"Since then I kept it at my farm until August, 1907, when I presented the stone to H. R. Holand."[19]

"The Stone, as I remember, was about 30 inches long, 16 inches wide, and 7 inches thick, and I recognize the illustration on page 16 of H. R. Holand's History of Norwegian Settlements in America, as being a photographic reproduction of the Stone's inscription."[20]

As Darwin Ohman, Olof's grandson wrote:

"There were scholars who accused my grandfather of forging the stone and inventing many of the runes unknown to scholars at that time. There was never a doubt in our family that this accusation was ridiculous. We knew Olof had not created a hoax. The local people in Kensington never had a doubt either. The Minnesota State Geologist, Newton Winchell, made three different trips to Kensington after 1909, and talked with Olof several times. He interviewed locals and reported that he believed Olof was an honest man, and concluded that the Kensington Rune Stone was a genuine historic artifact."[21]

However, at the time, disgusted with all the trouble the stone had caused, Ohman tossed the slab, inscription side down, in front of his granary door where it would act as a doorstep for the next nine years.

---

[19] See Chapter 5
[20] From Olof Ohman's affidavit (July 20, 1909);
[21] Darwin Ohman

CHAPTER 3

THE INSCRIPTION

The Stone's inscription actually reads like an abbreviated news article; summing up the basic facts, with the only element missing being the *why* of it.

The face of the stone:

Edge of the stone:

As stated in the previous chapter, when Professor O. J. Breda first translated the inscription in 1899, he believed the rune characters for the numerals, never having seen their like before, to be concocted fabrications to make the inscription look good.   In this initial translation Breda simply left these spaces blank, along with a couple of the words he didn't recognize, so that it came out as follows:

--- Swedes and --- Norwegians on a discovery-journey from Vinland west --- we had camp --- --- --- one day's journey north from this stone. We --- --- fished one day. When we came home found --- red with blood and dead. A.V.M. save from ---"

"--- have --- men by ocean to look after our ships --- day's journey from this island. Year ----

While incomplete there was just enough to whet the imagination; could it be possible that Vikings had actually explored the interior of the United States 130 years *before* Columbus even landed in San Salvador?

The Saga of Erik the Red and *The Greenlanders Saga* tell of the two landing sites, Straumfjord and Hóp on an unknown land west of Greenland. But is this the extent of the Viking exploration?

The lure of rich natural resources in the vast country just across the sea must have been irresistible, even though the price for them often proved to be high. Within only a few years two of Leif Erickson's brothers, Thorvald and Thorstein had died in their quests and greed had turned his sister, Freydis, into a murderer.

But if the inscription on the stone *is* genuine it means *someone* did return. And if so, this fact would throw into disarray *all* the neatly established timelines of European contact with the Americas; rewrite all the history books; a proposition some scholars cannot conceive or contemplate, even to the present day.

When the inscription was sent to European scholars in 1899, instead of giving it the study it was due they just doubled over in laughter, waving off the entire idea. When they examined the two tracings of the Stone they were sent, one of the scholars happened to notice they differed somewhat[22] and snidely suggested that the Siverts copy was probably the template from which Olof worked. Detractors immediately jumped on this offhand statement as being a scientific conclusion with but one meaning: the inscription was a hoax *"by a farmer who knew of runes from an old book."* (Of course, no one bothered to look into when the books on runes had actually been purchased by Ohman, which was almost a year *after* the stone was found.)

But a minor faux pas of this nature didn't matter; by declaring the inscription a fake and insinuating Olof was its creator the academics saved face and avoided any and all embarrassment and possible questioning of their professional judgment. Of course, they also did the world at large a disservice, but hey, what's that compared to holding on to one's precious reputation?[23]

---

[22] Which is the reason the second tracing was made

[23] I did not include the names of the scholars because even if I did, their contributions to science were negligible and they are long forgotten today. Yet the Stone is still finding its way into the news.

It's interesting that the scratched out runes and the Siverts copy (neither of them actual evidence of anything) are often touted to be just that and were enough to discredit Olof Ohman and create the groundless conclusion that he had carved the stone himself. A number of other scholars, perhaps believing they were being fair and unbiased, then jumped to conclusions about the language of the runes and their authenticity. They accused Olof of forging the stone and even "inventing" runes unknown to them[24] at that time. However, there was never a doubt in the Ohman family that this accusation was ridiculous; they knew Olof had not created a hoax, and the local people in Kensington who knew Ohman never had any doubts either.

Why *did* Olof gouge out the inscription with a nail, scratching the stone?

First of all, initially he had no idea of what the stone was (it could have just as easily been an old boundary marker left by an earlier settler) besides, the inscription was packed solid with soil that broke any wooden stick small enough to fit into the runes; an iron nail was exactly the size and type of object that was needed to clean them out. Olof couldn't possible have predicted how much this innocent act would contribute to the misunderstanding and rush to judgment that overtook common sense in the years to come.

Had the stone been found by a person of any other nationality and profession then approached with even an ounce of the objectivity science supposedly holds itself to, it would have been accepted as genuine over a century ago.[25]

In 1907, Hjalmar Holand[26] made his own translation, this time adding what he believed to be omitted words in square brackets:[27]

[We are] 8 Goths [Swedes] and 22 Norwegians on [an] exploration-journey from Vinland through [or across] the West [i.e., round about the West]. We had camp by [a lake with] two skerries one days-journey north from this stone. We were [out] and fished one day. After we came home [we] found 10 [of our] men red with blood and dead. AV[e] M[aria] save [us] from evil.

"[We] have 10 of [our party] by the sea to look after our ship [or ships] 14 days-journey from this island [in the] year [of our Lord] 1362.

While I understand the missing words in Professor Breda's translation, I believe Holand went a bit overboard in supplying and explaining his, inserting such un-needed verbiage as "round about the West".

---

[24] An excellent book which absolutely destroys the rune argument is *"The Kensington Stone is Genuine"* by Robert A. Hall, Jr. Although a bit tedious to read, he leaves no doubt about the authenticity of the inscription

[25] Only because Ohman was Swedish and a stone mason by trade was it questioned in the first place

[26] See Chapter 4

[27] Taken from *"Westward from Vinland"* (1940) page 101

I then made a verbatim, line by line, word by word translation of the Kensington Stone from the runic into modern Swedish then into English as follows:

Kensington : Stone :
Modern Swedish
English

8 : gøter : ok : 22 : norrmen : pa :
8 goterna och 22 norrman pa
8 Goths and 22 Norsemen on

opdagelse : fard : fra :
upptackt fram fran
discovery-journey through from

winland : of : west : wi :
Vinland genom vast vi
Vinland to west we

hape : låger : wep : 2 : skjar : en :
hade lager med 2 skar en
had camp by 2 skerries one

dags : rise : norr : fra : dena : sten :
dagsresa norr om denna sten
days-journey north from this stone

wi : war : ok : fishe : en : pagh : aptir :
var vi och fiskade en dag efter
we were and fished one day after

wi : kom : hem : fan : 10 : man : røde :
vi kom hem fann 10 man roda
we come home found 10 men red

af : blod : og : ded : AVM :
av blod och dod. AVM
with blood and dead AVM

fraelse : af : illu
radda fran det onda
Save from evil

Etched on the stone's side:

har : 10 : mans : we : hawet : at : se :
har 10 man vid havet att se
have 10 men by sea to look

apter wore skip 14 pagh rise
efter vara shis 14 dagar resan
after our ship 14 days journey

fram dena on ahr 1362
fran on ar 1362
from island year 1362

As one can plainly see, the modern Swedish translation, in many areas, is almost an exact replica of the stone's inscription. As the person inscribing the stone would naturally do so in their native language, the conclusion is obvious; the inscription was carved by a Swede (Goth).

I present the translation without editing or punctuation:

8 Goths and 22 Norsemen on discovery journey through from Vinland to west we had camp by 2 skerries one days-journey north from this stone we were and fished one day after we came home found 10 men red with blood and dead AVM Save from evil.

Have 10 men by sea to look after our ship 14 days-journey from island year 1362

Although the words are separated by what we call a colon in English, where the sentences actually begin and end is not designated, but was probably assumed to be obvious by the inscriber(s).[28] And we all know about the word assume.

My only argument with Holand's translation is that once he settled upon what he believed to be the correct sentence structure, he never questioned it. For my taste there are just too many bracketed words of Holand's own making. In fact, from the first time I read his translation I found the wording of the second, third and fourth sentences particularly curious:

"We had camp by 2 skerries one days-journey north of this stone. We were and fished one day. After we came home..."

---

[28] It is now believed the first five lines were chiseled by one person, the rest, including the edge, by another

[26]

Put in this manner, however, the third sentence doesn't make sense; there seems to be one or more words missing between *were* and *fished.* Most translations I've seen, like Holand's, simply supply the "missing" word in brackets, making the sentence read *"We were [out] and fished one day."*

I believe the inscription was translated correctly by Holand in 1907 after he found the evidence for runic numerals (heretofore forgotten by the academic community) but I believe he erred in the sentence structure. This is the way it should be read:

8 Goths and 22 Norsemen on [a] discovery-journey through from Vinland to west. We had camp by 2 skerries. One days-journey north from this stone we were and fished one day. After we came home, found 10 men red with blood and dead. AVM (Ave Maria) Save [us] from evil.

Have 10 men by sea to look after our ship 14 days journey from island. Year 1362

From ten words in brackets to two, and I altered nothing but the punctuation. The difference is significant, especially in the second, third and fourth sentences. And the reason for the altered the sentence structure is because when the English words *"we were"* is translated into Swedish, the "we" and "were" switch places to read *"One day's journey north from this stone **were we** and fished"*. (This makes Holand's translation read like a question ***"Were we** [out] and fished one day?"*) By simply ending the second sentence at the word "skerries" and starting the third with "One" the inscription suddenly reads more intelligently, requiring only one bracketed word in the final phrase *AVM fraelse af illu* (Ave Maria - Latin for Hail Mary) *Save [us] from evil.*

In Modern Swedish the final phrase translates to: AVM radda fran det onda. In modern Norwegian: AVM redde fra det onde. Both of which are similar to each other but neither of which is even close to the stone's inscription. It's only in Icelandic we find: AVM vista fra illu. This suggests the second person inscribing the stone was from Iceland.

In fact, entire phrases are used in reverse order when translating from the Scandinavian languages into modern English. For example, "I will go to the store" would be written "Go to the store I will." If the rephrasing is "corrected" the inscription reads like this:

8 Swedes and 22 Norwegians on a journey of discovery through the west from Vinland. We were one day's journey north from this stone [when] we made our camp by 2 rocky islands and fished one day. After we came home [we] found 10 men red with blood and dead. AVM Save [us] from evil.

14 days journey from [this] island [we] have 10 men by sea to look after our ship. Year 1362.

"Americanized" in this manner it now reads easier without any change in the meaning. The inscription on the side almost looks like an afterthought, explaining where they were headed and giving the date.

Careful reading of the next sentence tells us why no remains to date have been found: "We had camp by (*not on!*) two skerries."

This means that the party made camp on the *mainland* at a place where the two rocky islands were clearly visible. If so, then this could also explain the ease of the attack (although not its viciousness).

The Native Americans in that area at that time were the Sioux. When the Vikings split up to go fishing, the Sioux took advantage of the situation. This leaves little doubt that the Vikings had been watched as they sailed down the waterways but were probably unaware of it.

Also, the attack on their camp has the feel of retaliation (for an earlier confrontation never recorded?) We'll probably never know. Whatever the actual facts are, the Stone *does not* tell the complete story.

CHAPTER 4

THE DETECTIVES

Perhaps no one has been a stronger proponent for the Kensington Stone than the Norwegian-born amateur historian, Hjalmar Rued Holand (above). Although born in Holand, Norway, on October 20, 1872, at age 13 he, along with his older sister, Helene, immigrated to Chicago in 1885, where they stayed with an older brother and his wife. However Holand became dissatisfied with the living arrangements and was taken in by another sister who was living in Wautoma, Wisconsin, Annette Johnson. In 1898 he received his BA from the University of Wisconsin, earning his MA the following year. Holand eventually bought a farm near Ephraim, Wisconsin, where he would spend the remainder of his life.

Although he championed the Stone's authenticity, Holand and Olof Ohman would soon be at odds. It all began in August of 1907, when a young Holand was traveling through Minnesota giving lectures on Norwegian history. When talking to people after his lectures he *"found that the most vivid memory of former days which the people there had to relate was the discovery of this runic stone. As I had spent much time while in college in the study of runes and Old Norse, the story of this find interested me greatly. It was therefore with eager expectancy that I hunted up the owner of the stone and asked to see it.*[29]

"Out in the farm yard he showed me a large, dark colored stone lying near the granary door, half sunken in the ground.

"There was no inscription on the upper side, but the farmer turned the stone over. This under side presented on the whole a very smooth appearance with but few fractures, and the inscription which there appeared was technically a most excellent piece of work.

---

[29] From "Westward from Vinland" (1940) by Hjalmar Holand - pages 99-100

Most of the lines were evenly spaced and the characters were of almost uniform height – about one inch.

"The neat inscription continued for about three-fifths of the length of the stone. Although the characters were dark and weathered, they were quite distinct except in the lower left hand corner of the inscription. Here the characters were almost worn away. The inscription continued on the flat edge which did not have the natural smoothness of the face of the stone and showed evidence of having been trimmed smooth with a cold chisel. Here too, the inscription covered three-fifths of the length of the stone. Evidently the lower uninscribed part of the stone was intended to be placed in the ground.

"My wonder increased when I saw he length of the inscription. It is one of the longest of all runic inscriptions. I counted 220 characters, besides 62 double dots which were used to separate the words. Evidently the writer of this strange inscription was an artist in paleography who had a long story to tell."

Holand wanted to barrow the Stone to study it but at first Ohman was reluctant to let it leave with him. Right from the beginning to two men didn't click; something about Holand's personality didn't sit right with Olaf. After considerable pestering Ohman finally allowed Holand to take possession the Stone, but only on the condition that he *"deposit it on Ohman's behalf in the Minnesota Historical Society"*.

Instead, Holand simply kept the stone, even carving his own initials in it. In fact, his own writing betrays his true thoughts on ownership when he stated: *"Although I assumed that the inscription was spurious, inasmuch as it had been condemned by several scholars, I persuaded the owner to let me take it home with me thinking it would be an interesting souvenir[30] and exemplification of my favorite subject of study."[31]*

From the moment he got his hands on the Stone, Holand considered it his.

Darwin Ohman, Olof's grandson, stated on his website: *"Holand borrowed the stone from my grandfather in 1907, as a young scholar and wanted to do research on it. He was asked by Olof more than once to return it and Holand refused. It was never returned and eventually ended up with a group of businessmen in Alexandria, MN, where it still resides today. The last attempt by my grandfather to obtain the stone from Holand was a letter, from a lawyer representing the family, sent to Holand who lived in Wisconsin. Holand's response was that Ohman should come to Wisconsin and sue him. Obviously my grandfather did not have that kind of money."*

Ignoring or dismissing Olaf Breda's and George Curme's conclusions out of hand, Holand personally studied the stone, finally declaring the inscription authentic, insisting it was an actual Nordic rune stone from 1362, which he then proceeded to skillfully link to the Paul Knutson expedition of that year.

---

[30] Meaning he had no intention of ever returning it.
[31] From "Westward from Vinland" (1940) by Hjalmar Holand – pg. 100

Holand soon discovered the Rune Stone wasn't the only ancient Scandinavian object found in the continental United States. In June of 1871, 27 years *before* the Stone was turned up, farmer Ole Jevning, in Climax, Minnesota, while digging a hole for a fence post, unearthed a fire-steel about two feet below the surface. *"It was much rusted and there was also some charcoal and ashes."* It was later found to be identical to those at the University Museum in Oslo, whose director wrote to Holand, saying, in part, *"Upon request I will state that the fire-steel which carries the same mark in its entire form with the spiral ends is of exactly the same type as the fire-steels which in great numbers have been found in Norwegian graves from the Viking age..."*[32]

In 1878 a 14th century iron battle axe was discovered by a prospector in a riverbed 35 miles outside of present day Marquette, Michigan. *"...he reached down to pick the axe up from the bottom of the stream on which it rested, but upon grasping the handle or piece of the haft which protruded, the wood seemed to dissolve."*

What remnants of wood remained in the haft were later analyzed and found to be sub-arctic spruce, well known in northern Canada and Norway. For the spruce to become fragile enough to dissolve when grasped, it is estimated the axe had to have lain in the streambed for at least three hundred years.

Hjalmar Holand took a photograph of the axe head and compared it to one now resting in the Lillchammer Museum in Norway. He found that they were not just similar, they were *exactly* alike. In fact it's now believed that both came from the forge of the same Norwegian blacksmith.

Then, in 1894, five miles southwest of Evansville, Julius Davidson was pulling tree stumps on his land, when, as his wife described *"...he found a heavy axe of strange shape, the like of which he had never seen before. The top of the stump under which the axe was found was more than two feet in diameter, and my husband said it must have several hundred years old. The axe lay quite deep in the hole, about a foot and a half below the surface of the ground."*

A one of identical type can be seen in the hands of St. Olaf carved on the reredos from Østeråker (originally from Storkyrkan in Stockholm) now in the National Historical Museum. And in Minnesota, other Viking implements had turned up.

In 1899, farmer Nils Windjue's plow turned-up a fifteen inch long iron spear head on his farm in Sjuggerud coulee, Trempealeau county, Wisconsin. (It was actually Nils' five year-old son George that first saw it.) Holand later found the Folk Museum in Lund, Sweden, had about a dozen of exactly the same type.

When made aware of these finds (and others), it was proof enough for Holand that the inscription on the Stone was real, especially since all the implements had been found *years before* the Rune Stone came to light.

By late 1909, Holand's enthusiastic campaigning for the stone led the Minnesota Historical Society to delve further into the matter and in early 1910 they assigned State

---

[32] Eivind S. Engelstad, Oslo, September 18, 1928

Geologist Newton Horace Winchell to investigate. However, Olof Ohman did not speak a word of English and Winchell did not speak any Scandinavian languages, therefore Winchell hired Holand to translate. (Interestingly, Winchell's diary verifies that a hostility existed between Holand and Ohman even then. This is understandable; Holand now had had the Stone for two years and continued delaying Ohman about its return.)

In July of 1909, affidavits about the discovery of the stone were taken from Olof Ohman, Nils Flaaten, Roald Benson, Samuel Olson, and Edward Ohman (now 21) in Kensington, Douglas County, and the statements were witnessed and notarized.

Meanwhile that summer, Winchell made three different trips to Kensington, examining the discovery site, talking with Olof on several occasions, and interviewing witnesses in and around the area. He interviewed locals and finally reported that he believed Olof was an honest man, and concluded that the Kensington Stone was a genuine historic artifact.

Winchell also interviewed livery man Joseph Horvedt who was the first person to suggest that Ohman carved the stone, in the process telling Winchell *that you can't go much by what I say because I'm always contrary."* Winchell commented that Horvedt was *"the only man I have found who doubts the authenticity of the stone."* Winchell then interviewed several others who all agreed that Horvedt was unreliable.

This photo was taken at a ceremony in July of 1909. Olof Ohman is in the center.

Around 1900, R. Anderson wrote a newspaper article claiming that A. Anderson, a neighbor of Olof's, had "implied with a wink" that Ohman had carved the runes. The article went on to state that Ohman knew *of* runic writing and had an interest in history.

A. Anderson immediately replied with a letter to the editor denying the claim, saying that he'd only replied to the reporter's question, saying *"perhaps it **could** have been done."* Olof Ohman quickly wrote to Newton Winchell denying the story.

About this time Swedish linguist, Otto von Frisen, declared the inscription a hoax saying, *"The inscription is fabricated in modern time by a man who was partly acquainted with runes but where this partial knowledge failed, he created himself new characters."*•

This was in reference to the runic numerals which would later be revealed in use in medieval times. However, the linguists studying the Stone in 1909-1910 were not yet aware of them. When brought to light, however, the "mystery runes" suddenly became a powerful argument for the Stone's authenticity; for, if experts in the runic field didn't know anything about them, then how could a 19th century stone carver?

Then, in December of 1909, Olof, through translator Samuel Olson, approached Winchell and told him that the stone had not been given to Holand as his personal property, as Holand was leading everyone to believe. Through Olson, Ohman personally told Winchell to keep the stone and not allow Holand to take it. However the Stone was actually in the hands of the Minnesota Historical Society who believed Holand was its owner and refused to let Winchell take possession of it.

In January of 1910, linguist Prof. O.J. Breda declared the inscription a hoax and comments, *"and the language! That it was not Old Norse was clear at a glance!"* (He is later proven wrong.)

By the spring of 1911 Holand, now openly claiming the Stone was *his* property, offered to sell it to the Minnesota Historical Society for $5,000. If the deal went through Holand pledged that Olof Ohman would get $100. But, with questions about its veracity now causing uncertainty, the Society elected not to buy it and instead returned it to Holand. Holand then traveled to Europe with the rune stone that summer where he was rejected by the scholars there using the same arguments as in the United States.

The situation cannot be summarized any better than by the letter Newton Winchell wrote to Holand:

My Dear Holand,

I have only just now read the account in the Norwegian American, of your lecture at the University of Christiana, and your reply to the criticisms of Hagstad on the inscription. I am struck with the similarity of the case in Norway with the early stage of the discussion in America. In both countries they cite certain evident variations from the high literary style of the date of 1362. In America these have been examined into and no longer offer stumbling blocks, in the acceptance of the record, but in Norway they have advanced no further than these linguistic stumbling blocks. Hagstad's whole argument is about on a par with Flom's and has no more force. It remains for some philologist in Norway (whom Hagstad seems to call a "scientist"), who has not in precipitate judgment already condemned the stone, to dispassionately and thoroughly investigate it.

The repetition of the old objections which have been sufficiently removed in America may at first blush before an audience which is not well informed on this special question, appear sufficient to disprove the inscription, and in Norway, as in America, may carry the day temporarily against the stone. But it is quite likely that, after a little time given to more detailed study by some experts, the truth will appear to be on the side of the rune stone. I do not consider the result of the Norway meeting, even as reported by some of the old enemies of the stone in our American papers, as fatal, or even as seriously damaging to the stone, for the same stage of the investigation has been passed through in America.

Further, there are certain topographical and physical elements in the case, and in my judgment these weigh so strongly and fundamentally in favor of the stone that it appears to be that the little linguistic irregularities must be made to stand aside or be explained in conformity with these elements. A certain ancient king is said to have given the orders that the tide of the ocean should not advance so as to disturb him. I have no doubt that his hearers proclaimed him great and applauded his wisdom; but it is also said that the king was obliged to remove from his place or be overwhelmed by the superior force that carried the great tide. So with the rune stone, as it appears to me, and as it appeared to be when I first gave attention to it, and I stated in my first paper concerning it - there are geological (physical) aspects of the question (which absolutely require that the stone's story be correct). These are fundamental and cannot be set aside by verbal technicalities such as are, to this date, brought up to disprove it. They stand impregnable while a light combat rages about them among the scouts. When the line of battle reaches these fundamental truths they will assert their power. No one has, as yet, attacked those important bulwarks of the rune stone. They are discussed in the report of the Museum committee of the Minnesota Historical Society.

Still, even as the discussion now stands the... technical linguistic difficulties are apparently removed by your dignified reply to Prof. Hagstad published in the same number of the Norwegian American. The only lingering uncertainty lies in the word opdagelse. - i.e. whether it could have existed in 1362 under the primitive form opdage, else being a terminational and unobjectionable suffix.

The elementary state of the discussion in Norway is amusing and at the same time vexing, because it goes out to the "Verdict of Norway." On the contrary it is only the loud blast of the first onset of the opponents of the stone who, having already announced their views (viz. Bugge and Hagstad), make a show of bravery in standing by their posts. The same took place in America, where similar loud blasts were found to consist almost wholly of noise, and gave the stone more help than harm once the smoke blew away.

Again, it is quite amusing to read of Hagstad's statement that the stone is composed of a soft material. On the contrary, it is harder than granite, standing next to pure

Holand held onto the stone until the Alexandria Chamber of Commerce finally offered him $4,000 (none of which went to Ohman) and they are still the stone's current owner.

In 1914, Professor William Hovgaard, using ancient Nordic documents, deduced that "a day's journey" or *daer sigling* (day's sailing) was equivalent to approximately 75 miles. Armed with this information, Holand, in the summer of 1919, personally took it upon himself to see if there was actually a lake or river containing two skerries in the direction and at the distance indicated in the inscription.

Holand's search took him north from Douglas County to Becker County and, after a considerable search, to Cormorant Lake which, much to his satisfaction, has two small rocky islands. Rowing out to the islands Holand discovered a boulder on each island that had been drilled with triangular hole, about seven inches deep, in which he believed would fit an iron mooring pin. To him, the mooring stones confirmed the Rune Stone's authenticity and the inscription's story.

Holand claimed that because of the lake's odd kidney shaped outline, there was only one spot from the North shore where both islands were visible in the same line of sight and therefore announced that *this* must have been the site of the attack. (Cursory excavations found nothing. And the two islands *are* visible from the entire length of the Eastern shore of the lake, one but has to turn their eyes slightly to look at one then the other. Why Holand believed both islands had to be in the same line of sight is not understood.)

In 1916 Warren Upham of the Minnesota Historical Society visited the Ohman farm, and interviewed Olof at length. He left convinced that the stone was genuine and that Olof Ohman was an honest man. Upham, now a firm believer in the Stone's authenticity, then attempted to persuade the society to renegotiate with Holand and purchase the rune stone, but his efforts prove fruitless.

It wasn't until 1923 that Olof Ohman, who rightly still considered himself to be the stone's owner, received a letter from Holand stipulating that Holand would pay him 10% of whatever he received from selling the rune stone. Ohman was furious and again demanded the return of the stone but Holand refused and the tension between them mounted,

Upon the publication of Holand's first book "The Kensington Stone" in 1932 one last attempt was made by Olof (now in his 70s) to get the stone returned via a letter from a lawyer representing the Ohman family. Holand's curt response was that if Olof wanted it that bad he should come to Wisconsin and sue him for it. This was during the Great Depression and of course Olof simply didn't have that kind of money.

(Interestingly, Holand's home in Wisconsin burned to the ground in 1934 along with all of his notes, documents and photos he had gathered over the years regarding the rune stone.

Then, on August 27, 1935, Olof, age 80, died at home.

Holand went on to publish three more books about the stone; "Westward from Vinland" in 1940; "America 1355-1364: A New Chapter in Pre-Columbian History" in 1946; and "Exploration in America before Columbus" in 1956.

In 1948, Edward Ohman, now 50 years-old, gave an interview in which he dispelled the notion that the stone was ever used as a doorstop. He also said that he pounded an iron rod into the ground at the discovery site and hoped that a stone marker could be erected one day.

Actually, a movement had been started in Kensington as far back as 1927 to build a 204 foot monument at the site where the stone was discovered. As enthusiasm over the project grew, several large rallies were held to help raise the estimated $300,000[33] needed to complete construction. However the funding fell far short and the monument never proceeded beyond the planning stages.

A smaller 15 ft. monument was finally built in 1963 but, ironically, was erected in the wrong place. Today it sits between two roadways, the actual discovery site remaining unmarked and between 40 and 50 feet away.

In 1949 Karin Ohman, Olof's wife passed away. (Olof died in 1935.) Brothers Art and John still lived on the farm, and after their sister Amanda's husband died, she too returned to live with them.

In the fall of that same year, Johan A. Holvik, a professor at Concordia College, in Moorhead, Minnesota, visited the Ohman farm and interviewed Amanda, who showed

---

[33] Approximately $5 million today

him the family scrapbook. He asked to barrow it, as well as the Rosander Swedish Dictionary owned by the family, *"to help clear the Ohman family name."*

Amanda was hesitant but reluctantly agreed. Then, less than a week later she received a check from Holvik for five dollars along with a letter telling her to cash the check and that he would keep the books. The next day Holvik published a newspaper story in the Minneapolis Star in which he declared the rune stone was blank when it came out of the ground and that Olof inscribed it later.

Amanda immediately returned a $5 check, telling Holvik that the scrapbook was *never* for sale sell, she was only loaning it to him, and demanded that he return it. Holvik simply ignored the request.

Later that fall, Willie Sarsland, a neighbor of the Ohmans, came across the article. He quickly penned a letter to the Minnesota Historical Society saying that he was present just minutes after the discovery and not only saw the inscription on the stone, he, in fact, helped clean the dirt off. For reasons of their own the Society never sees fit to publish this information.

Meanwhile Amanda had contacted a lawyer who also sent a request to Holvik to return the books, but this too was ignored. By 1950 Edward Ohman had written Holvik twice asking that the book be returned, but this had no more effect than the previous letters. Edward passed away that December. Then, in early 1951 Swedish archeologist Erik Moltke wrote a series of articles attacking the inscription as a fraud and naming Olof as its perpetrator. Three months later, in April, unable to deal with the loss of her brother and the personal attacks on her family, Amanda hung herself. *"One can only imagine how much the Holvik incident and the loss of the precious scrapbook contributed to her grief."[34]*

This means, if indeed the scrapbook is still in the hands of the Historical Society, they have committed fraud against the Ohman family (for purporting that the book was returned when it was not) and theft, because they have stolen merchandise. Both charges would do serious damage to the reputation of the Society, which is why I conclude the entire segment of finding the article from the Swedish newspaper in the scrapbook garbage. (To prove otherwise all they have to do is provide a photocopied page from the scrapbook showing the article along with a written affidavit by a member of the Ohman family verifying its authenticity.)

After Holvik eventually died, the books wound up with the Minnesota Historical Society. According to the Society's records, the Ohman family scrapbook was returned to Art Ohman in the 1970s. Curiously, family members were never able to locate it after Art's death.

The final straw that broke the camel's back for the Ohman family came in the late 1960s when a film crew from the British Broadcasting Company (BBC) appeared on the

---

[34] Darwin Ohman

Ohman farm telling Art (the only offspring that remained on the farm until his death in 1974) they were doing a positive documentary on the Rune Stone. Instead, it portrayed the stone as a hoax. After that, whenever strangers would stop by and ask to see the site where it was discovered, Art refused to talk to them and just sent them on their way. Who can blame him?

In the past, the claims about the stone's legitimacy were almost often quickly countered by an army of historians desperate to prop up their preconception of the progression of New World exploration and settlement by Europeans, sighting the supposedly "modern grammar" found within the inscription.

Just as Robert A. Hall, Jr., had in his 1982 book *"The Kensington Stone is Genuine"*; Dr. Richard Neilsen in the spring 2001issue of *Scandinavian Studies* addressed the complaints directed toward some of the rune forms utilized throughout the 74-word message as being unavailable in the 14th century. Dr. Neilsen earned a doctorate of technology from the University of Denmark in Copenhagen in 1965; became fluent in Danish and began a nearly 40-year infatuation with Scandinavian cultures and languages, becoming fluent in Norwegian, Swedish, Finnish and Icelandic. As an employee of the Bechtel Corporation back in the States (1985-87), he continued to be sent back to the region three times per year and kept his languages fresh by examining and studying various Scandinavian artifacts and ancient writings in his spare time.

Within two weeks of his first examination of the Stone, Dr. Neilsen was able to eliminate one of the longest standing objections, the appearance in the inscription of the so called Arabic "10". Beginning with Prof. O.J. Breda at the University of Minnesota in 1899, scholars with their limited knowledge of rune forms available to 14th century Scandinavians had used this number "10" to bolster their contention that the inscription was a modern forgery.

Dr. Neilsen immediately pointed out that Scandinavians had translated a huge Arabic text on mathematics during the 1300s, thus knew about Arabic numerals, a fact then unknown to detractors. This served to pique Neilsen's interest in the Kensington Stone controversy and initiated a decade-long study of the stone and its fascinating message.

Neilsen, like Hall, took all of the criticisms of the "modern" runes and one by one showed in detail how each of the rune forms appear in ancient writings elsewhere across Scandinavia predating the supposed hoax inscription made in 1898, many of which were unknown to, or at least never utilized by, the critics.

CHAPTER 5

THE PAUL KNUTSON EXPEDITION

In 1362, the same date as on the Stone, King Magnus *"King of Norway, Sweden, and Skåne"* gave orders to Paul Knutson[35], at Anarm, to sail to a Knorr[36] to Greenland and from there to – wherever. The king not only desired to make sure Greenland was following the Christian religion, he wanted it spread where ever the Vikings went, including Vinland. Of course, being that Knutson was traveling in a cargo vessel, he might as well return with a prized load of lumber, especially the free red pine and white oak so prized and highly desired in the shipbuilding and furniture making trades. Out of the virgin forests it was not unheard of to obtain single boards three feet wide, two inches thick, and thirty feet long.

After the trees were felled, they were squared and split into boards of varying thickness using a wooden mallet and a tool called a froe. (This is all confirmed by archaeological evidence. Any waste wood that couldn't be sold was simply cut up and used as firewood.)

The squaring and splitting had several very practical purposes; pre-cut lumber was easier to sell by the piece; also cut timber could be stacked closer together than round logs, eliminating wasted space; and square beams and boards would not roll on the decks in heavy seas; the timber was simply easier to load and transport onto a Knorr *after* the trees were processed.

---

[35] See the last Chapter
[36] A cargo vessel - also Knarr; (in Icelandic – Knöörr)

But Knutson's 30 men were not just looking for timber; the almost unlimited supply of trees along the east coast alone precluded any necessity for exploring the interior of the country for it. The fact that many of the runes trace back to Gotland indicate the presence of Cistercian monks (the 8 Goths) who were very likely involved with the long-term plans of the group. In fact, they may have expected the wording in the first sentence *"8 Goths and 22 Norsemen"* to be automatically interpreted as "8 Cistercian monks accompanying a party of 22 Norsemen." Why else mention the ethnicity if they didn't expect it to explain who they were?

The Paul Knutson expedition had sailed from Iceland to America in two ships; the larger one, called a *Knöörr,* was used for transporting goods and even entire families on colonizing voyages, and featured a central platform where animals, wood, or other necessities could be stored and transported. Too large to navigate narrow rivers, it is undoubtedly a Knöörr that had 10 men guarding it by the sea *"14 days journey from island."*

The exploration party probably proceeded downriver in a *Drakkar,* which was perfectly suited for incursions. These ships were commonly between 17 and 27 meters long and 2.5 to 5 meters wide amidships; and even fully loaded a Drakkar drew less than one meter of water, giving the Vikings the ability to navigate all but the shallowest of rivers. The ship was even light enough to be dragged over land in order to circumvent a blocked river.

Depending on the Drakkar's size, although a dismountable mast and rectangular sail were used whenever possible, the ship could still require anywhere from 20 to 50 oarsmen. When wind was lacking, or when sailing up a river, the men took turns rowing. But this was an exploration party of only 40 men (subtracting the 10 that were left guarding the mother ship). They must have proceeded downriver in an even smaller ship, the type which were commonly used for fishing and would have been especially good for navigating small waterways, probably around 10 meters long and requiring only 10 to 12 oarsmen. (During their sailing from Iceland, the smaller vessel could have been easily towed behind a Knöörr.) One interesting characteristic shared by all Viking ships was an identical bow and stern. This meant that when they needed to turn back, the oarsmen simply turned around and rowed in the other direction.

From the Sagas, we conclude that only wealthy Vikings had sufficient capital for the construction of Drakkars and Knöörrs. Thus, ship owners usually were nobles, or commoners who had amassed great fortunes through trading or raids. The size, quality, and quantity of ships depended on the Viking's level of wealth. Accordingly, Vikings of lesser stature could only afford smaller ships suitable for fishing or short voyages.

Not only did the Norse tell of the Skræling people that they encountered over the centuries, but the aboriginals also tell of making contact with the Norse. The Inuit

(Eskimos) have a tale about a Kavdlunait (Inuit word for foreigner or European) that was speared by a Kayaker and how they feared revenge from the Kavdlunait because of the killing.

Violence was the usual interaction between the two people, inhibiting peaceful trade and any real successful settling of these areas by Viking explorers. Such stories are also mentioned in the Saga of Erik the Red and the Greenlander Saga written about 1220, about Thorvald and Thorfinn Karlsefni's attempt to settle in Vinland.

The Norse explorers pointed out that despite all of Vinland's natural resources they were under almost constant attack by the Skræling and any peaceful contact between the two people was simply not going to happen.

In 921 the Arab chronicler Ibn Fadlan met Rus traders of Swedish origin, near the Middle Volga. Impressed by the Viking's appearance he described them as *"perfect physical specimens, tall as date palms, blonde and ruddy."* He was also appalled by their apparent lack of hygiene as well as their uninhibited sexual practices. *"They are the filthiest of God's creatures. They have no modesty in defecation and urination, nor do they wash after pollution from orgasm, nor do they wash their hands after eating."*

I also have the definite feeling the stone doesn't tell the entire story; that there had already been an encounter between the two groups (possibly more than one) that didn't come off well for the Sioux, an intensely clean people. If so, it would explain the savage attack upon the Vikings – it was revenge. The 10 men left behind had no ship; and no immediate means of escape. They were sitting ducks.

And while the massacre of their men was the catalyst for carving and leaving the Stone where they did, its permanence suggests that it was actually a location marker; and the fact that they bothered to leave it at all means they fully expected a future Viking party to find and read it.[37]

One posited theory today is that the "ten men" were not attacked at all; that they actually died from disease, possibly bubonic plague.

Nonsense.

First of all the plague was, in fact, spread by the infected fleas on rats, and was unknown in the New World. All 30 men had been aboard the same Knorr together since sailing from Norway. Fleas are not a selective sort; had infected ones infested the ship, they would have bitten the Cistercian monks and Norsemen with equal abandon. And once infected: *"The infection spread to everyone who had any contact with the diseased. Those infected felt themselves penetrated by a pain throughout their whole bodies and, so to say, undermined. Then there developed on the thighs or upper arms a boil about the*

---

[37] It's also been suggested that *"stone holes in the area constitute a finding grid that is not an accident."* On this I have no comment.

size of a lentil which the people called a "burn-boil". This infected the whole body, and penetrated it so that the patient violently vomited blood. This vomiting of blood continued without intermission for three days, there being no means of healing it, and then the patient expired. Not only all those who had speech with them died, but also those who had touched or used any of their things."[38]

Finally, as the strain of plague rampaging through Europe during the 1300s killed within *48 to 72 hours* after one was infected, the men never would have made it as far as Greenland, much less the into the interior of the American continent. (Those who posit such theories should study a little medicine before making such unsubstantiated claims.)

Also, there is no logical reason to believe the stone is actually a ciphered runic puzzle as claimed by O. G. Landsverk in his book *Runic Records of the Norsemen in America.*. Without going onto his questionable methods of "decipherment" the idea of a lone priest traveling through the uncharted North American wilderness chiseling out encrypted puzzles that had no chance[39] of being found, and even if they were, no one understanding them, is rather absurd. He would have absolutely nothing to gain and everything, including his life, to lose.

Vikings, it must be remembered, carried weapons not just in battle, but also as symbols of their owners' status and wealth. Many were often decorated with fine inlays, twisted wire and other adornments in silver, copper and bronze. Laws from the late Viking period show that all free men were expected to own weapons, too. All wealthy entrepreneurs setting up expeditions were expected to provide them for their men.

The main offensive weapons were the spear, sword and battle-axe, although bows and arrows and other missiles were also used. The most common weapon in their arsenal was the spear. A forged iron blade mounted on a wooden shaft, usually ash, anywhere from 6 to 9 feet in length, used for both thrusting and throwing. The blade tips varied in shape from broad leaf shapes to long narrow spikes. It's been recorded skilled spearmen were able to throw two spears at once using both hands, and to even catch a spear in mid-flight then hurl it back with deadly effect.

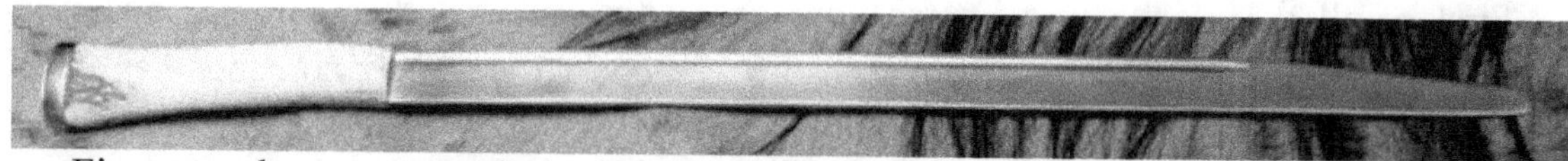

Fine swords were a symbol of high status, being very costly (and labor intensive) to make. The hand hammered iron/steel blades were usually double-edged and up to 90cm, or a little over, in length, although single-edged sabers (above) are known, and both were worn in leather-bound wooden scabbards.

---

[38] Excerpts from "Account from Messina"
[39] One's odds of hitting the lottery are better than a second Norwegian finding the stone in the American wilderness of the 1300s

Early sword blades were pattern-welded, a technique in which strips of wrought iron and mild steel were forged together, hammered to length, then twisted (which created the pattern in the metal) then hammered out again. Then, leaving a center ridge, the edges were carefully filed down, sometimes almost razor sharp. Later blades of homogeneous steel, imported from the Rhineland, bore inlaid makers' marks and inscriptions, such as INGELRII or ULFBERHT. Still, Viking craftsmen often added their own elaborately decorated hilts, and many swords were given names, such as Leg-biter and Gold-hilt.

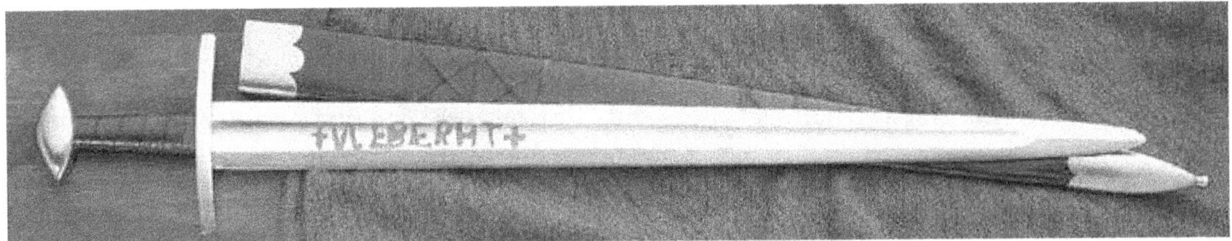

Long-handled battle-axes might be used instead of swords, particularly in open combat. The famed, double-handed broad axe is a late development, typical of the late 10th and 11th centuries. But as the owner could not hold a shield at the same time, he would take cover behind the front line of warriors, rushing out at the right moment to hew down the enemy.

Viking Ships represented the height of technology in their day. The Vikings were brilliant ship designers and builders, and as the needs of the warriors were different from those of the merchants, different ships were especially designed for both. All ships were built of red pine with strong oak keels, with *"thin overlapping planks fanning out to form the iconic, graceful hull – the gaps between the planks stuffed with animal hair and tar. The rudder was fixed on with a twisted birch sapling. Sails spun from wool."*

Knorr's were broader in proportion to their length than the warships (the largest known being 48 feet in length and able to carry up to 40 tons of goods). The typical length to width ratio was 3:1, making a Knorr broader in its proportion to its length, compared to warships, and providing them with a wider and deeper hull under the raised decks to hold cargo; animals, lumber, and all large items were stored above decks.

The ships were built in different sizes (the light freight-carrying vessels being called Byrding) and primarily used for transporting goods and/or even entire families on colonizing voyages. Since a Knorr could carry a great deal of cargo it had a deeper draft which made it unusable in shallow water.

A Knorr was also much more dependent on the sail than the oars, as, instead of speed, the real priority was to have a seaworthy vessel that could safely cross vast stretches of the North Atlantic Ocean. The oars were only used to help guide the ship in and out of port or if the ship was becalmed at sea.

To navigate rivers the Vikings needed lighter more maneuverable ships; vessels light enough to be pulled out of the water in order to portaged over shallows, waterfalls, or whatever other obstacles might impede their progress.

There were 3 Types of Viking warships: the Snekke, Drekkar, and Skeid. All 3 types had a shallow draft and were long[40] (90 feet in one case) and narrow. Drakkar (Dragon ships or longboat) were commonly between 50 and 80 feet long and 7 to 15 feet wide amidships making them fast and easy to steer. Although a dismountable mast and rectangular sail was used whenever possible, the larger Drakkar's required anywhere from 20 to 50 oarsmen.

Smaller Drakkar's were made for fishing and typically only required 10 to 12 men at the oars. Even fully loaded these vessels drew less than one meter of water, giving the Vikings the ability to navigate all but the shallowest of rivers. (The *Faering* was the smallest vessel, just a rowboat with two oars.)

Drakkar's were primarily built as a row boats, the oars providing dependable speed and maneuverability for difficult situations, and would have been the main type of ship the Vikings used in their surprise attacks.

Unfortunately we don't know exactly what type of ship was used by the men when exploring the river in 1362, but it was probably a Drakkar of some sort. The possibility of death on such ventures was taken for granted. If they made it back to the Knorr at Hudson Bay and returned to Greenland, no one found the journey exceptional enough to record it.

---

[40] Hence the term "longboats"

CHAPTER 6

THE GEOLOGY

The Kensington Stone is a piece of solid greywacke[41] approximately 31 inches high by 16 wide and 6 inches thick, weighing 202 pounds. (About five percent of the stones around Kensington are greywacke.) The slab was split from a flat piece of rock (the tool marks of a cold-chisel are still visible) that was deposited in the area by glacial ice anywhere from 12-15,000 years ago as attested to by the scratches (several up to ¼ inch in depth) on the reverse side of the stone, vertical to its length, from glacial ice passing over the slab when it was still a part of the bedrock. The lower left hand corner of the face of the stone is covered with a deposit of white calcite with a number of the runes chiseled into this softer rock and now practically illegible except by help of context and are much more legible on the photographs than on the stone itself.

W.O. Hotchkiss, the state Geologist of Wisconsin, was the first to submit his findings to the Minnesota Historical Society in March of 1910:

"I have carefully examined the various phases of weathering on the Kensington Stone, and with all respect for the opinions of philologists, I am persuaded that the inscription could not have been made in recent years. It must have been made at least 50 to 100 years ago and perhaps earlier unless some artificial process was used to produce the weathered appearance."

Next, in an eleven page report dated April 21, 1910, Geologist Newton Winchell submitted his, which reads in part:

"Resolved, that this committee renders a favorable opinion of the authenticity of the Kensington Rune Stone, provided that the references to Scandinavian literature given in this committee's report and accompanying papers be verified by a competent specialist in the Scandinavian languages."

"The said stone is not a modern forgery, and must be accepted as a genuine record of an exploration in Minnesota, at the date stated in the inscription."

---

[41] An extremely dense stone, being next to pure quartzite in rigidity, harder even than granite

The said stone is not a modern forgery, and must be accepted as a genuine record of an exploration in Minnesota, at the date stated in the inscription.

N. H. Winchell

Dr. Warren Upham, an eminent glacial geologist, also examined of the stone in 1910 and wrote:

"When we compare the excellent preservation of the glacial scratches, shown on the back of the stone, which were made several thousand years ago, with the mellow, time-worn appearance of the face of the inscription, the conclusion is inevitable that this inscription must have been carved hundreds of years ago."

In a letter to Hjalmar Holand dated August 17, 1911, Newton Winchell stated: *"The changes of physiography are such that no faker could have wrought them into such an inscription within the last 100 years."*

In a further statement prepared for publication in the Journal of American History (vol. IV, 180) Newton wrote: *"I am convinced from the geological conditions and the physical changes which the region has experienced, probably during the last 500 years, that the stone contains a genuine record of a Scandinavian exploration into Minnesota, and must be accepted as such for the date named."*

It is interesting to note that no known eminent geologist has published any documentation critical of Winchell, Hotchkiss, or Upham within the last 100 years. Only Erik Wahlgren attempted to impugn the validity of Winchell's 1910 report in 1958 *"alleging that it was virtually dictated by Holand."*[42] (This was quickly proven to be groundless.)

Most geologists have simply refused to study the Stone as a result of the widely held and widely publicized negative opinions of the philologists.

In 1926 Professor O.E. Hagen, then a well-known Assyriologist, who had a highly developed skill in determining the genuineness of cuneiform tablets by their patina and weathering, began a study of the Kensington Stone. Unfortunately, before he could complete his work his home was destroyed by fire. Hagen survived, but not without some serious bodily injuries. Sensing he was not long for this world Hagen penned a letter to

---

[42] The Kensington Stone is Genuine – Robert A. Hall, Jr., - pg. 62

his friend, one W. Ager, editor of the Eau Claire, Wisconsin, newspaper "Reform". The letter, which follows, was printed in full in the April 19, 1926 edition.

"All my notes concerning the discussion of the Kensington Stone also became a prey to the flames. This loss I felt so much more deeply as I, some time ago, publicly announced that I would make known my views concerning it. As the circumstances are now I cannot attempt any exhaustive dissertation, and for the present I can only make the following categorical statement.

"In epigraphic respects I find in the inscription no evidence that it is anything except what it purports to be. I worked over the stone for a whole day under different kinds of light and found the runes on the whole to be what I looked for from that time and the people that are mentioned in the inscription.

"In linguistic respects the inscription presents certain peculiarities, perhaps also errors in writing, but real philological errors showing it to be a forgery I do not find. The negative side of this protracted discussion concerning the authenticity of the inscription has, however, often made use of assertions and argumentations, which to speak as mildly as possible, must be stamped as scientific irresponsibility. It is not disputed that the inscription is before us as a comprehensible document and it therefore behooves the negative side to present actual valid evidence to show that it is a forgery. Such evidence, in my opinion, has not yet been presented. On the contrary there has been found in the Kensington region a number of remarkable finds which in a surprising manner seem to corroborate what the inscription relates.

"My advice is therefore that the Kensington Stone be placed in a safe repository where it can be preserved as an important epigraphic document concerning American history."

O.E. Hagen

Just as Hjalmar Holand had become the Kensington Stone's most ardent proponent, Erik Wahlgren emerged as the stone's principal antagonist. In 1952 Wahlgren, having come across the 1949 article, wrote to Holvik asking to see the Ohman family scrapbook, as well as the Rosander Swedish Dictionary Amanda had given him. A few weeks later he published a paper highly critical of the rune stone listing a number of arguments, none of which are regarded as valid today. (In fact, Linguists attacking the stone, only to be discredited later, becomes an all too familiar pattern in the Stone's history.)

Walter Gran of Kensington was the son of John Gran. In a 1972 interview Walter claimed that on his deathbed his father had "confessed" to him alone that the rune stone was a fake and that he and Olof Ohman had carved the inscription. Even though there were no witnesses to the event and few around Kensington believed Walter, many mentioning his tendency to "exaggerate," the story caught on. A subsequent interview with Gran in 1975 showed him to not have a coherent story. A jury would never have bought it, but there was no jury. The rune stone and Olof were convicted of fraud without a trial. The "deathbed confession" suited the anti-stone atmosphere of the times and fit the template of a hoax that the hungry media had adopted.

In 1975, Theodore Blegen published his book, "The Kensington Rune Stone: New Light on an Old Riddle." Blegen also claimed Olof had carved the stone and even though his version events contradicted Gran's, both were somehow regarded as correct.

Interviews are conducted with eight elderly Kensington residents in 1981; people who knew Olof, John Gran and others who were there at the discovery. *All of them* said they did not believe Walter Gran's claim that his father had admitted carving the stone with Ohman because they regarded Olof as too honest to have been involved in a hoax. However, for some reason none of the positive testimony's held any sway in the public opinion at large and the rune stone's fate was sealed.

In July of 2000, Luann Patten of the Rune Stone Museum contacted Scott Wolter of American Petrographic Services and asked him to conduct a forensic analysis of the Stone, keeping with strict scientific procedure. Wolter, who had never heard of the Kensington Stone prior to being contacted, thus allowing him to conduct the project with no preconceptions, then convened a panel of prominent geologists at Petrographic to design and agree upon a peer reviewed[43] methodology of the Stone's evaluation, and settle the weathering question once and for all. Scott Wolter, Texas engineer Dick Nielsen, archeologist Alice Kehoe and other members of Wolter's team concluded that in the end the study confirmed the 1910 work of Newton Winchell - that the carvings are at *least* several hundred years old. Their 30-page report issued in November concluded with these words:

"It is clear that the four man-made fracture surface types on the Kensington Rune Stone exhibit weathering (primarily mica degradation) consistent with being buried in the ground for at least decades and probably centuries. This being the case, the logical conclusion is that the Kensington Rune Stone is an authentic artifact, presumable made at the time it is dated (1362 A.D.)."

"It changes history in a big way." Wolter stated. *"In my mind the geology settled it once and for all."*

The majority of geologists who have examined the Stone over the years have either gone on record in favor of its authenticity or adopted a wait-and-see attitude, while linguistic academicians (with rare exceptions such as Hall) simply repeat the initial errant conclusions of their forebears. American Petrographic's did extensive microscopic examination of the Stone and their 30-page APS report concluded with these words:

---

[43] This is in sharp contrast to other studies done by single persons which were not reviewed at all.

"It is clear that the manmade surface types on the Kensington Rune Stone exhibit weathering (primarily mica degradation) consistent with being buried in the ground for at least decades and probably centuries. This being the case, the logical conclusion is that the Kensington Rune Stone is an authentic artifact, presumably made at the time it is dated."

The Kensington Rune Stone is a piece of 2 billion year-old meta-greywacke indigenous to Minnesota. Across its reverse side there are two, white, roughly ½" wide, undulating and branching lines which were produced by prolonged contact with the aspen tree roots. Such scars on rock are relatively common and are produced when a fungus in the ground and the acid from the root combine and leach nutrients from soil and rock as food for the tree. As this is a process that *only* takes place over decades of constant exposure to the elements it must be taken as further evidence of the inscription's true age.

The root-leaching pattern matches perfectly with the three sketches made by Olof Ohman in 1909, Sam Olsson in 1910 and Olof Ohman Jr. in 1957, as well as the testimony of the twelve witnesses who signed written affidavits.

American Petrographic's also performed a weathering study using chip samples collected (with permission) from biotype-rich slate tombstones from a cemetery in Hallowell, Maine; an area with a very similar climate and weathering patterns as in Kensington. Their studies concluded that, primarily due to the mechanical processes of wetting and drying, and the yearly freeze-thaw cycle, after about 200 years the mica minerals had begun to wear away from the carved surfaces of the tombstones.

On the Kensington Stone's carved surfaces they found the mica breakdown was even more pronounced, meaning the Stone's inscription dates to more than 200 years prior to 1898, because, aside from the 7 years it spent in the Ohman's barn yard, the Stone hasn't been in a weathering environment since.

It was Winchell, in 1909 who first noted in his report that Olof told him (through translator Hjalmar Holand) that he took a nail and scratched out the inscription which was still packed with mud. The nail crushed the minerals at the bottom of the grooves which then turned white giving the inscription a "fresh" appearance to the untrained eye. However, microscopic inspection shows the walls of the grooves exhibit extensive weathering,[44] the pyrite evidence consistent with the original inscription being older than 26 years at the time it was discovered. However, the mica tombstone study further served

---

[44] This can be seen with the naked eye also, it one but takes the time to study the Stone.

to prove the weathering is consistent with the inscription being far older than 200 years from 1898, all but eliminating the concept that the inscription is fraudulent.

Another recent example of erroneous theory was offered by a geologist who claimed the white calcite on the face side of the Kensington Rune Stone (and dozen or so runes carved into that area) would have dissolved away by exposure to acidic water if it had been shallowly buried on the hill at the Ohman Farm. What he failed to do was actually take samples from there. If he had, he would have discovered the area has a higher than neutral pH (<7) meaning it would *"quickly neutralize any acidic solution produced by the decomposition of the organic material and not attack the calcite. In fact, it actually promotes the accumulation of secondary calcite as found on the bottom back end of the artifact."*

In 2001 a boulder inscribed with runes was discovered near the Ohman Farm which turned out to be a prank inscription made by archaeology students at the University of Minnesota in the summer of 1985. The boulder was tested and found to contain pyrite of the same size as in the Kensington Stone, and actively weathering pyrite crystals were found within the carved grooves of the boulder.

Pyrite, an iron sulfide, is present in greywacke stones like this, and is a mineral that weathers relatively quickly in the presence of water and oxygen. When it weathers it becomes iron oxide. Many small pits along the walls of the grooves are lined with iron oxide deposits produced when exposed pyrite crystals weathered away. The question became: *"How fast does pyrite deteriorate to iron oxide in an environment like that to which the Kensington Stone was exposed, and can that be used to date the cut and carved surfaces?"*

As of the summer of 2010, the pyrites in the prank inscription were still actively degrading. When compared with the pyrite pits within the Kensington Stone's grooves, the conclusion was that the Kensington Stone's inscription was subject to weathering for far longer than 25 years. Since the stone has been protected from weathering since 1907, and in order for the pyrite to have so completely eroded in the inscription, it had to have weathered for at *least* a century before it was discovered in 1898. One can only conclude that on the geologic evidence alone the Kensington Stone *cannot* be a 19th century hoax.

I have primarily dealt with the geologic aspects of the Stone for one reason: if the inscription is proven to have weathered more than 100 years (before Europeans came to the Kensington area of Minnesota) then the Stone is genuine; the best arguments of the linguists are moot. What runes or words they believe were or weren't used in 1362 becomes a matter of opinion, not fact, and quite frankly, after proving the inscription's age their *opinion* does not (and should not) matter.

Studying the inscriptions on tombstones of known ages and comparing the weathering to that on the Kensington Stone proves conclusively the Stone saw centuries

of exposure to the elements after being inscribed and before falling face-first onto the soil. The weathering alone, which could not be faked at the time the Stone was found, tells us it is authentic.

Instead of being mired down with inane arguments about Scandinavian grammar; pointless speculation about the Knights Templar (give me a break!), runic puzzles, forgers, and all the rest of the nonsense, we should be looking at the stone as a valid documentation of an actual event.

Today, the National Museum of Natural History continues to receive public inquiries about the Stone and the Smithsonian's current position. The Department of Anthropology answers these inquiries with a statement written in unambiguous terms saying that "in its scholarly opinion the Smithsonian has judged the Kensington Stone to be a nineteenth-century creation."

CHAPTER 7

THE SMITHSONIAN

Although specialists such as Olaf Breda and George Curme had dismissed the Kensington Stone as a fraud, by the late 1940s a campaign by Hjalmar Holand brought it considerable public support. With a Nudge from the Wisconsin congressional delegation, the Smithsonian put the Stone on exhibit from 1948 to 1953. Upon examining it in 1949 Dr. M.W. Stirling, Director of the Bureau of American Ethology at the Smithsonian wrote: "The Kensington Rune Stone is probably the most important archeological object yet found in America."

Those present at the opening included (left to right) Waldo R. Wedel, Curator of Archaeology at the Smithsonian, Representative Andersen of Minnesota, Sidney Dean Sarff of the Minnesota State Society, and John E. Graf, Acting Secretary of the Smithsonian. Today the Smithsonian sides with the majority of Nordic language scholars who believe the stone is a modern creation.

As a result, several archaeologists and linguists criticized the Smithsonian for mounting a "misleading display" creating ensuing controversy because of which in 1951 the Institution commissioned a new study of the stone by the Danish ethnologist William Thalbitzer. Thalbitzer was a highly respected elderly scholar, but his specialty was Eskimo ethnology, not archaeology or runes. His study resulted in qualified support for the authenticity of the runes, yet the Institution, for reasons that had more to do with internal politics than strict archaeology, failed to give it their unqualified support. In a news release of September 23, 1951, the institution stated in a press release that "the

Smithsonian has taken no position with regard to its authenticity, but felt that its presence in Washington would provide runic scholars a further opportunity to study it."

The Smithsonian's neutral position sparked even more controversy in the academic community (which was, by this time, solidly against the Stone's authenticity). The continuing controversy soon led to the appearance of a critical review by Brønsted in 1954, published by the Smithsonian, and two books, one by Moltke in 1953 and a second "The Kensington Stone: A Mystery Solved" by Eric Wahlgren (University of Wisconsin Press, 1958), all of which took decisive stands based on detailed studies of the history and circumstances of the find. Wahlgren's analysis in particular makes a plausible case for a late nineteenth century rune stone hoax in the Scandinavian-settled area of Minnesota, sighting that in remote rural areas of Norway and Sweden knowledge of runes was not an esoteric academic discipline in the nineteenth century; in fact runic script was alive and well. Olof Ohman (who had *an interest in history, folk knowledge of runes, and a sense of humor"*) himself came from Forsa in the neighboring province of Halsingland, a community where runes were still being used up until the 1920s thus, in Wahlgren's mind, was the probable perpetrator.

[What I find most curious is the fact that in the article from the *Swedish newspaper Post och Inrikes Tidningar* dated December 13, 1867 which described a rune stone dated *"1612 found in Vadstena, Sweden, clasped by the roots of an ash tree"* there is no doubting *its* authenticity. Wait a minute; this stone was found in a country where literally hundreds of people knew runes, and its genuineness was never questioned. Yet, in the United States, where outside the Academic community *almost no one* knows anything about runes, when a stone is unearthed in exactly the same conditions it's immediately labeled a hoax! Why?!]

"Although many rural people were illiterate in regular reading and writing, knowledge of runes was widespread. Runic forms changed from one generation to another, and it is revealing that some of the runes on the Kensington Stone are of an eighteenth- to nineteenth-century variety used in Dalecarlia, the province of Ohman's mother. Ohman admitted knowing runes and had been seen carving runes on sticks during his early years in Minnesota.

"Among the articles found pasted into Ohman's scrapbook, now in the Minnesota Historical Society, is one from the Swedish newspaper Post och Inrikes Tidningar dated December 13, 1867. It describes a rune stone of 1612 found in Vadstena, Sweden, clasped by the roots of an ash tree. The article mentions how the stone was shown to be one hundred and fifty years old by a count of the tree's growth rings.

"According to a neighbor of Ohman's, Jonas P. Gran, the runic inscription was planned long in advance of its finding and may have been inspired by this newspaper story. In tape recordings (also held by the Minnesota Historical Society), Gran said that the inscription had been composed by Ohman and his friend, Sven Fogelblad, a former Lutheran minister, and that Ohman and Gran did the actual chiseling. Ohman and Gran

buried the stone under the roots of a small ash and then waited for a good opportunity to retrieve it. Both Gran and Ohman enjoyed pranks and, according to Gran, they enjoyed the commotion that resulted."

As stated in Olof's sworn statement *"I emigrated [sic] to America in the year 1881, and settled upon my farm in Section 14, Township of Solem, **in 1891**."*

*"In the month of **August, 1898**, while accompanied by my son Edward, I was engaged in grubbing upon a timbered elevation, surrounded by marshes, in the southern corner of my land, about 500 feet west of my neighbor's, Nils Flaaten's house, and in full view thereof."*

As Olof did not even move into the area until 1891 and didn't find the stone until 1898, we are to believe, then, that an aspen tree (not ash!) was to grow to 10 inches in diameter in only 7 years – making the tree rings literally over 1 inch apart – fantastic growth by any measure.

Also, *all* trees have tap roots which grow straight down, unless obstructed, it which case they will grow around the obstruction and continue down into the earth. If the stone had been placed under a sapling, its root would have already formed going straight down. Even if bent around the stone, it would still display a full three dimensional growth; meaning the root would still be *round*, not *flattened* on one side.

Of course, these are all arguments of common logic.

Then, in early 2000, the book "Vikings: The North Atlantic Saga" was published by the Smithsonian in which one chapter expends three full pages describing the Stone as a hoax. That spring Michael Zalar responded to the book by publishing an article in The New England Antiquities Research Association's journal listing "37 factual errors" in the book, including the deliberate attempt to misrepresent the 1910 report by State Geologist Newton Horace Winchell on the inscription's weathering.

Wolter's team documented every individual rune on the stone with a microscope and discovered dots inside four R shaped runes on the stone. Believing they were intentional and meant something, Wolter and Nielsen scoured rune catalogs.

"We found the dotted R's. It's an extremely rare rune that only appeared during medieval times. This absolutely fingerprints it to the 14th century. This is linguistic proof. This is medieval, period." Wolter said. *"It makes me ask the question if they were wrong about that what else were they wrong about?"*

Still some linguistic experts claimed the runes on the Stone were made up, such as the two rune's in the form of an L and a U which are crossed which they say should not be - even after Nielsen located them in an old Swedish rune document dating back to the 1300s.

Not able to find argument with the geologic evidence, the detractors kept coming back to the same tired old statements about the runes – even after they were answered!

CHAPTER 8

THE BIOLOGICS

By the time Erik the Red homesteaded Greenland the Viking and the Skræling had long known of each other's existence. Around 900 AD the Thule (ancestors of today's Inuit and originally from Siberia) began expanding across the Canadian Arctic, spreading into Northern Greenland shortly after the Vikings had settled there. As the Thule moved south along the coast they came in violent contact with Norse settlements, sometimes annihilating them.

When Thorvald Erikson landed in Vinland sometime around 985 his 50 member party began setting up a fortified camp at Hóp (Point Rosee). It is recorded that *"almost as soon as the Norsemen hauled their longboats onto the beaches fighting broke out with the local natives."*

The Norsemen were not in the least surprised by the "welcoming comities" awaiting them; both peoples were already well known to each other, and further proof of the interaction between the two groups was found in two different sources.

Around 2005, Agnar Helgason, a scientist at Iceland's deCODE Genetics, began investigating the origin of the Icelandic population. To no one's surprise most of the people he tested carried genetic links to either Scandinavians or people from the British Isles. But then he found a small group of Icelanders, roughly 350 in total, carried a lineage known as C1, usually found only in Asians and Native Americans.

"We figured it was a recent arrival from Asia," Helgason said. *"But we discovered a much deeper story than we expected."*

Helgason's graduate student, Sigridur Sunna Ebenesersdottir, found that she could trace the matrilineal sequence to a date much earlier than when the first Asians began arriving in Iceland. In fact, she found that all the people who carry the C1 lineage are descendants of one of four women alive around the year 1700. In all likelihood, those four descended from a single woman. And because archeological remains in what is Canada today suggest that the Vikings were in the Americas around the year 1000 before retreating into a period of global isolation, the best explanation for that errant lineage lies with an American Indian woman: one who was taken back to Iceland some 500 years before Columbus set sail for the New World in 1492.

"Quantitatively, the importance of the discovery is fairly minimal," says Carles Lalueza, a researcher at Barcelona's Institute of Evolutionary Biology, who collaborated on the project. *"You're talking about a few people on a remote island. But qualitatively, the fact that there is evidence for the transmission of genes between two continents at that early a date is very exciting."*

And it's not just the mere fact of contact that is intriguing. Until now, the historical evidence has suggested that while the Vikings may have reached the Americas, they didn't really engage with the indigenous population. *"According to the sagas, the Vikings had troubles with the locals and couldn't settle there, so they returned to Iceland,"* says Helgason. *"But if we're right, it will mean they didn't just sail there and come back. They had real contact with them."*

Yet in "The Saga of Erik the Red" chapter 12, it states: *"Snorri, Karlsefni's son, was born the first autumn, and he was three winters old when they began their journey home. Now, when they sailed from Vinland, they had a southern wind, and reached Markland, and found five Skrælingar; one was a bearded man, two were women, two children. Karlsefni's people caught the children, but the others escaped and sunk down into the earth. And they took the children with them, and taught them their speech, and they were baptized."*

The story of an American Indian female taken on a Viking ship to Iceland now had a basis in recorded fact. To prove it beyond question will require finding the same genetic sequence in older Amerindian remains elsewhere in the world — family members, as it were, most likely in Iceland. Helgason and his team hope that as news of their finding spreads, other geneticists will re-examine remains they have already studied for evidence of the same lineage.

In the meantime, Helgason is exploring one other possible explanation for the unexpected finding. Though unlikely, the presence of the C1 lineage could indicate that it originated in those ancient populations who dispersed from Europe into Asia and the Americas. In other words, instead of a single American Indian carrying the lineage to Europe, it may have risen out of primitive Europe and migrated to different parts of the world. *"If that's the case, we'd be talking about 14,000 years ago,"* says Helgason. *"So even if we're wrong about this one Amerindian woman, the other answer would be even more spectacular."*

I believe the stone was left as a memorial to their fallen comrades; but a mass grave containing 10 Norwegian explorers just a few feet below the earth where the stone once sat is highly unlikely. (If remains are found however, it would not only validate the stone once and for all, it would make all the varied speculation over the inscription meaningless.)

CHAPTER 9

THE SAGAS

Included here are two texts that tell of the discovery of the Americas, followed by the letter from Magnus to Paul Kuntson.

The Sagas were first put onto paper in the original Icelandic around 1220 and not translated into English until 1880 by J. Sephton. One problem with his translation was in the Scandinavian sentence structure (as noted on the inscription on the stone) which to English readers, tends to reverse some of the words and even phrases, making some sections difficult to read, even confusing. There are also archaic verbal references (such as in the Greenlanders Saga where they talk about *the good and the good*) which, not having a modern reference, I have left as written. Without changing the context, in 2018 a modern translation of the 1880 version was made by this author, including, when known, the present-day names of people and places.

Also, between the two sagas there is a wide discrepancy of spelling of what appear to be the same names. I have decided to leave them as they are because, quite frankly, I do not know which is correct and which is not (nor is it really that important to the story).

The Sagas largely complement each other, giving some of the same information, and in my mind, may have started out as a single tale which, through a secession of tellers over the centuries, became split into two. However, there are some differences; in The Greenlanders Saga, it is a man named Bjarne Herjulfson who becomes lost in the fog and discovers the American continent; in The Saga of Erik the Red it is Leif Erikson who makes the same journey.

To me, The Greenlanders Saga is the original version, later adapted by those in Erik the Red's camp and modified slightly to make his family's achievements more exceptional. Again, this is just my opinon. Enjoy.

The Saga of Erik the Red
(Eiríks saga rauða)

Chapter 1

Olaf, who was called "Olaf the White", was styled a warrior king in Norway. He was the son of King Ingjald, the son of Helgi, the son of Olaf, the son of Gudrid, the son of Halfdan Whiteleg, king of the Uplands.

Olaf led a harrying expedition of sea-rovers into the west, conquering Dublin and Dublinshire in Ireland, over which he made himself king. He married Aud the Deep-minded, daughter of Ketil Flatnose, son of Bjorn the Ungartered, a noble man from Norway. Their son was named "Thorstein the Red".

Olaf fell in battle in Ireland, and then Aud and Thorstein went into the Sudreyjar (the Hebrides). There Thorstein married Thorold, daughter of "Eyvind the Easterling", sister of "Helgi the Lean" and they had many children.

Thorstein became a warrior king and formed an alliance with Earl "Sigurd the Great", son of "Eystein the Rattler". They conquered Caithness, Sutherland, Ross, and Moray, and more than half of Scotland. Over these Thorstein was king until the Scots plotted against him and there he fell in battle.

Aud was in Caithness when she heard of Thorstein's death, upon which she ordered a merchant-ship to be secretly built in the forest and when she was ready directed her course out into the Orkneys. There, she gave "Thorstein the Red's" daughter, Gro, in marriage, who became mother of Grelad, whom Earl "Thorfinn the Skullcleaver" married.

Afterwards Aud set out to seek Iceland. Having twenty free men in her ship Aud came to Iceland and passed the first winter in Bjarnarhofn (Bjornshaven) with her brother Bjorn. Afterwards she occupied all the Dale country between the Dogurdara (Day-meal river) and the Skraumuhlaupsa (river of the Giantess's Leap), and dwelt at Hvamm. She had prayer meetings at Krossholar (Cross-hills), where she caused crosses to be erected, for she was baptized and deeply devoted to the faith. There came with her to Iceland many men worthy of honour, who had been taken captive in sea-roving expeditions to the west, and who were called bondmen.

One of these was named Vifil. He was a man of high family and had been taken captive beyond the western main and was also called a bondman before Aud set him free. When Aud granted dwellings to her ship's company Vifil asked why she gave no abode to him like unto the others. Aud replied that, "It was of no meaning to him," she said, "for he would be esteemed in whatever place he was, as one worthy of honour." She gave him Vifilsdalr (Vifilsdale) and he dwelt there and married. His sons were Thorbjorn and Thorgeir, promising men, and they grew up in their father's house.

There was a man named Thorvald, the son of Asvald, the son of Ulf, the son of Yxna-Thoris. His son was named Eirik. Father and son removed from Jadar (in Norway) to Iceland, because of manslaughters, and occupied land in Hornstrandir, and dwelt at Drangar.

There Thorvald died and Eirik then married Thjodhild, daughter of Jorund, the son of Atli, and of "Thorbjorg the Ship-breasted", whom afterwards Thorbjorn, of the Haukadalr (Hawkdale) family, married. It was Thorbjorn who dwelt at Eiriksstadr, near Vatzhorn, after Eirik removed from the north.

Then did Eirik's thralls (slaves) cause a landslide on the estate of Valthjof, at Valthjofsstadr, that killed a prized race horse. "Eyjolf the Foul", Valthjof's kinsman, slew the thralls beside Skeidsbrekkur (slopes of the race-course), above Vatzhorn. In return Eirik slew "Eyjolf the Foul" and also "Hrafn the Dueller" at the Leikskalar (playbooths). Gerstein, and Odd, of Jorfi, kinsman of Eyjolf, were found willing to follow up his death by a legal prosecution; and then was Eirik banished from Haukadalr.

Eirik then occupied Brokey and Eyxney, two islands in the mouth of the fjord, and dwelt at Tradir, in Sudrey, the first winter. At this time did he lend to his neighbor Thorgest several pillars for seat-stocks, Afterwards Eirik removed into Oxney, built a farm and dwelt at Eiriksstadr. He then claimed his pillars, and got them not. Then Eirik personally went and fetched the pillars from Breidabolstadr (Breidabolstead), and hearing of it Thorgest came after him. They fought at a short distance from the hay-yard at Drangar, and there fell two sons of Thorgest, and some other men.

After that both Eirik and Thorgest kept a large body of men together guarding their farms. Styr gave assistance to Eirik, as also did Eyjolf of Sviney, Thorbjorn Vifilsson, and the sons of Thorbrand of Alptafjordr (Swanfirth). Giving assistance to Thorgest were the sons of Thord Gellir, as well as Thorgeir of Hitardalr (Hotdale), Aslak of Langadalr (Longdale) and Illugi, his son.

The case was tried at the Thorsnessthing session, (with "The Saga of the Ere-Dwellers" revealing the details), such as there was a huge crowd and that Styr was Eirik's "special helper" (council) in court. Styr did what he could to plead Eirik's case, but in the end the court outlawed Eirik. Eirik left. Styr then begged Snorri, the Chief, not to help Thorgest's men pursue Eirik after the session. For this favor Styr promised to help Snorri if he should ever be in trouble. Afterward, Thorgest's men found Eirik's ship ready to sail in Eirik's Bay. With many ships Thorgest began hunting for Eirik among the islands in the bay even as Eirik was being hidden by his friend, Eyolf, in Dimunarvagr (Dimun's Bay).

Eirik said to his people that he purposed to seek for the land which Gunnbjorn, the son of "Ulf the Crow" saw when he was driven westwards over the ocean and discovered Gunnbjarnarsker (Gunnbjorn's rock or skerry). He promised that he would return to visit his friends if he found the land. Thorbjorn, Eyjolf, and Styr accompanied Eirik beyond the islands. They separated in the friendliest manner, Eirik saying that he would be of the like assistance to them, if he should be able to be so, and they should happen to need him.

Then Eirik sailed ocean wards under Snæfellsjokull (Snowfall Glacier) and first sighted Greenland at the glacier called Blaserkr (Black-sark). Then he journeyed south along the coast to see if there were any inhabitants of the country and trying to find a livable spot, rounding the southern tip.

He passed the first winter at Eiriksey (Eirik's Island), mid-way to the Vestribygd (Western Settlement). The following spring he proceeded to Eiriksfjordr (Eirik's fjord) and taking land for himself fixed his farm there. During the summer he explored the unpeopled districts in the west, and was there a long time, giving names to the places far and wide. The second winter he passed at Eirik's Holm in Eiriksholmar (Eirik's Isles), off Hvarfsgnupr (peak of disappearance, Cape Farewell) near the southern tip of Greenland. The third summer he went altogether northwards, to Snæfell (Snowfell) and into Hrafnsfjordr (Ravensfirth). Coming to the head of Eiriksfjordr, he turned back and passed the third winter in Eiriksey (Eirik's Island) at the mouth of Eiriksfjordr.

The next the summer he sailed back to Iceland and landed at Breidafjordr (Broadfirth). This winter he spent with Ingolf, at Holmlatr (Island-litter). During the spring he and Thorgest fought again but this time Eirik met with defeat. Afterwards they reconciled their differences, allowing Eirik to return to the land he had discovered the next summer, which he called Greenland, *"Because,"* he said, *"men will desire much more to go there if the land has a good name."*

Eirik tried to persuade others into settling in Greenland with him by telling them it was richly endowed with nature's gifts, such as seals, whales, walruses, bears, and other wild game.

It is said twenty-five ships sailed from Broadfjord and Borgfjord in Iceland that summer but only fourteen reached Greenland. Some were driven back, others lost at sea. Eirik built his home at Brattahlid (Steep-slope) in Eirik's fjord. That was fourteen or fifteen years before Christianity was made the law in Iceland.

Chapter 3

Thorgeir Vifilsson married and took for a wife Arnora, daughter of Einar from Laugarbrekka (the slope of the hot spring), the son of Sigmund, the eon of Ketil-Thistil, who had occupied Thistilsfjordr. The second daughter of Einar was named Hallveig. Thorbjorn Vifilsson took her for a wife, and received with her the land of Laugarbrekka, at Hellisvollr (the cave-hill). To that spot Thorbjorn moved his home and became the temple-priest, great and worshipful, with a magnificent estate. Thorbjorn's daughter was Gudrid, the fairest of women and of peerless nobility in all her conduct.

There was a man named Orm, who dwelt at Arnarstapi (eagle-rock), who had a wife named Halldis. He was a well-to-do franklin and a great friend of Thorbjorn; Gudrid lived at his house as his foster-child for a long time.

There was a freedman named Thorgeir who dwelt at Thorgeirsfjall (Thorgeir's fell) who was mighty rich in cattle. He had a son whose name was Einar, a handsome man, well-mannered and a great dandy. Einar, at this time was a travelling merchant, sailing from land to land with great success and always passing his winters in either Iceland or Norway.

Now, one autumn after this, when Einar was in Iceland, he proceeded with his wares along Snæfellsness (Snow-fell farm) with the object of selling. He came to Arnarstapi and Orm invited him to stay there. Einar accepted his invitation because he and Orm's people were very friendly, and his wares were taken into a certain outbuilding. There he unpacked his merchandise and showed it to Orm and the housemen, and asked Orm take from them such things as he would. Orm accepted the offer and pronounced Einar to be a goodly gallant traveler, and a great favorite of fortune. Now when they were busy with the wares, a woman passed before the door of the building.

Einar inquired of Orm who that fair woman might be, passing before the door. *"I have not seen her here before."* He said.

"That is Gudrid, my foster-child," said Orm, daughter of Thorbjorn the franklin, from Laugarbrekka.

"She must be a good match," Einar said; *"surely she has not been without suitors who have made proposals for her, has she?"*

"Friend, proposals certainly have been made," Orm replied, *"but this treasure is not to be had for the picking. She is known to be particular in her choice, as well as her father, also."*

"Well, in spite of that, she is the woman whom I have it in my mind to propose for," said Einar, *"and I wish that in this suit of mine you approach her father on my part and apply yourself, pleading diligently for me, for which I shall pay you in return a perfect friendship.*

"The franklin, Thorbjorn, is a man in a position of great honour and owns a fine abode, but I am told his personal property is greatly on the decrease. He may reflect that our families would be suitably joined in the bonds of affinity. For neither I nor my father lack lands or personal property and if this alliance should be brought about the greatest assistance would accrue to Thorbjorn."

"Of a surety I consider myself to be your friend," Orm replied, *"and yet am I not willing to bring this suit forward, for Thorbjorn is of a proud mind and overall a very ambitious man."*

Einar replied that he desired no other thing than that his offer of marriage should be made known. Orm then consented to undertake his suit, and Einar journeyed south again until he came home.

Thorbjorn, awhile after, then had a harvest-feast as he was bound to have because of his great rank. Orm, from Arnarstapi, was present along with many of Thorbjorn's other friends. Orm entered into conversation with Thorbjorn and told him how that Einar from Thorgeirsfjall had been to see him lately and was becoming a promising man. He now began the wooing on behalf of Einar, and told Thorbjorn that an alliance between the families would be very suitable on account of certain interests.

"It just might happen, franklin, you could benefit greatly from this alliance."

But Thorbjorn answered, *"I did not expect the like proposal from you! That I should give my daughter in marriage to the son of a slave! And so you perceive that my substance is decreasing?! Well, then, my daughter shall not go home with you, since you consider her worthy of so poor a match!"*

Then Orm returned home and each of the other guests to his own household; but Gudrid remained with her father and stayed at home that winter.

In the spring Thorbjorn made a feast to his friends, and there came many guests and the banquet was of the best. During the banquet Thorbjorn called for a hearing and said: *"I have dwelt here a long time. I have experienced the goodwill of men and their affection towards me and I consider that our dealings with one another have been mutually agreeable.*

"But now my money matters do begin to bring me uneasiness, although at this time, my condition has not been reckoned contemptible. I wish, therefore, to break up my household before I lose my honour; to move from the country before I disgrace my family. So now I purpose to look after the promises of Eirik the Red, my friend, which he made when we separated at Breidafjordr. I purpose to depart for Greenland in the summer, if events proceed as I could wish."

These tidings about his future plans appeared to the guests to be important, for Thorbjorn had long been beloved by his friends. They felt that he would have only made so public a declaration so that there would be no point in attempting to dissuade him from his purpose. Thorbjorn then distributed gifts among the guests and then the feast was brought to an end, and they departed to their own homesteads.

That summer Thorbjorn sold his lands and bought a ship which had been laid up on shore at the mouth of the Hraunhofn (harbor of the lava field). Thirty men ventured on the expedition with him, including Orm, from Arnarstapi, and his wife, and those friends of Thorbjorn who did not wish to be separated from him.

They launched the ship and set sail with a favorable wind, but when they came out into the open sea the favorable wind ceased and they experienced great gales and made an ill sped voyage throughout the summer. In addition to that trouble there came fever upon the expedition and Orm died, along with his wife Halldis, and half the company. Then the sea became rougher and they endured much toil and misery in many ways and only managed to reach Herjolfsnes, in Greenland, at the very beginning of winter.

At Herjolfsnes there lived the man named Thorkell, a useful and most worthy franklin. He received Thorbjorn and all his ship's company for the winter, assisting them in right noble fashion. This pleased Thorbjorn well and his companions in the voyage

Chapter 4

At that time there was a great dearth (deficiency of food) in Greenland; those who had been out on fishing expeditions had caught little, and some had not returned at all.

In the settlement there was a woman named Thorbjorg. She was a prophetess (witch) and was called Litilvolva (Little Sybil). She had had nine sisters, and they were all witches but she was the only one now living.

During the winter it was the custom of Thorbjorg (as Litilvolva) to make a circuit of the settlement. People gladly invited her to their houses, especially those who had any curiosity about the upcoming season or desired to know their fate. Inasmuch as Thorkell was chief franklin of the area, he considered that it was his duty to know when the scarcity which overhung the settlement should cease. He therefore invited the prophetess to his house, and prepared a hearty welcome for her. As was the custom wherever a reception was accorded a woman of her kind, a high seat was prepared for her and a soft cushion of poultry-feathers was laid upon it.

That evening Thorbjorg arrived dressed as the witch Litilvolva, and accompanied by the man who had been sent to meet her. She was dressed in a blue mantle with strings for the neck and inlaid with gems all the way down to the skirt. Around her neck she wore glass beads, and over her head, a hood of black lambskin lined with ermine. She had a staff in her hand with a knob ornamented in brass and inlaid with gems. She wore a girdle of soft hair around her waist, and therein was a large skin-bag in which she kept the talismans needful to her in her wisdom. She wore hairy calf-skin shoes on her feet, with long and strong-looking thongs to them, and great knobs of latten at the ends. On her hands she wore gloves of ermine-skin with the white fur *inside*.

When Litilvolva entered the room all men saw it as their bounden duty to offer her greetings, which she received according to the men that were agreeable to her. The franklin, Thorkell, took the wise-woman by the hand and led her to the seat prepared for her. He then requested that she cast her eyes over his herd, his household, and his homestead. She did, but remained altogether silent.

The tables were set; and now I must tell you what food was made ready for the prophetess. There was prepared for her porridge of kid's (baby goat's) milk and the hearts of all kinds of living creatures were found and cooked for her. She had a brazen spoon, and a knife, its point being broken off, with a handle of walrus-tusk, on which was mounted two brass rings.

When the tables were removed, the franklin Thorkell advanced to Litilvolva and asked her how she liked his homestead and the appearance of the men. Also, he wanted to know how soon she would ascertain that which he had asked and which the men desired to know. She replied that she would not give an answer until the next morning, after she had slept there for the night.

The next night, when the day was far spent, the preparations which she required for the exercise of her enchantments were made for her. Litilvolva begged them to bring to her those women who were acquainted with the lore needed for the exercise of the enchantments, who knew one of the "weird-songs" needed for the ritual, called Warlocks. But no such women came forward. Then a search was made throughout the homestead if *any* woman were so learned.

Then Gudrid answered, *"I am not skilled in deep learning, nor am I a witch-woman, although Halldis, my foster-mother in Iceland, taught me the lore which she called Weird-songs."*

"Then you are wise and in good season." answered Litilvolva.

"But that secret lore and the ceremony are of such a kind that I want no part of," Gudrid replied, *"because I am a Christian woman."*

"You can offer your help to the men in this company and yet be none the worse woman than you were before." answered Litilvolva. *"Thorkell, I hereby give you charge to provide the things that are needful."*

Thorkell then urged Gudrid to consent until she finally yielded to his wishes. It was only then the women formed a ring around the scaffold and Litilvolva ascended to the seat and prepared for her enchantments. Then Gudrid sang the weird-song Warlocks in so beautiful and excellent a manner that to no one there did it seem that he had ever before heard the song in voice so beautiful as now. The prophetess then thanked her for the song.

"Many spirits have been present under its charm," Litilvolva said, *"even those who before would turn away from us and grant us no such homage were pleased to listen to the song."*

"Now many things are clear to me which before were hidden both from me and others and I am able to say this: that the dearth will last no longer; the season improving as spring advances; and the epidemic of fever which has long oppressed us will disappear quicker than we could have hoped."

"And you, Gudrid, I will recompense straightway. For that aid of yours which has stood us in good stead, and because your destiny is now clear and foreseen to me. You shall find a match[45] here in Greenland, a most honorable one, though it will not be a long-lived one for you, because your way lies out to Iceland. There shall arise from you a line of descendants both numerous and goodly, and over the branches of your family shall shine a bright ray."

"And so now, happily fare thee well, my daughter."

---

[45] Leif Eriksson

Then a visitor from another homestead came after Gudrid and she went there. Thorbjorn was also invited because he did not wish to remain at home while such heathen worship was being performed. The men then went to Litilvolva one by one and each inquired after what he was most curious to know. She was liberal in her replies - and what she said proved true.

Once spring began the weather soon improved as Litilvolva had predicted. Thorbjorn made ready his ship and sailed on until he came to Brattahlid. Eirik received him with the utmost cordiality, saying he had done well to come there. Thorbjorn and his family stayed with him during the winter and in the following spring Eirik gave land to Thorbjorn at Stokknes, and handsome farm buildings were built there for him and he dwelt there afterwards.

Chapter 5

Eirik had a wife who was named Thjodhild, and two sons; Thorstein, and Leif and an illegitimate daughter, Freydis. She was married to Thorvard and lived with him at Garar, which is now the Bishop's Seat. She was a proud and haughty woman, and Thorvard a narrow minded weakling. These sons of Eirik were both promising men. Thorstein was then at home with his father and there was at that time no man in Greenland who was thought so highly of as he. In those days the people of Greenland were still pagan. Leif had sailed to Norway, and was there with King Olaf Tryggvason.

Now, when Leif sailed from Greenland during the summer, he and his men were driven out of their course to the Sudreyjar (Hebrides). They were slow in getting a favorable wind from this place and they stayed there a long time during the summer. Here Leif grew fond of a woman named Thorgunna. She was of good family, and, as Leif discovered, not without some knowledge of secret lore. He finally reached Norway about harvest-tide.

Leif joined the body-guard of King Olaf Tryggvason, and the king formed an excellent opinion of him, and it appeared to him that Leif was a well-bred man. Once upon a time the king entered into conversation with Leif, and asked him, *"Do you purpose sailing to Greenland in summer?"*

Leif answered, *"If it is your will, I should wish to do so."*

"I think it may well be so." The king replied. *"You shall go on my errand and preach Christianity in Greenland."*

Leif said that he was willing to undertake it, but that, for himself, he considered that message a difficult one to proclaim in Greenland. But the king said that he knew no man who was better fitted for the work than Leif.

"And you shall carry good luck with you in it." The king said.

"That can only be," said Leif, *"if I carry **your** luck with me."*

Leif set sail as soon as he was ready. He was tossed about a long time out at sea, and lighted upon lands of which he had no expectation. There were fields of wild wheat, and the vine-tree in full growth and they gathered samples of all this. There were also the trees which were called maples, some trunks so large that they were used in house-building.

Leif came upon men who had been shipwrecked, and took them home with him, and gave them sustenance during the winter. Thus did he show his great munificence and his graciousness when he brought Christianity to the land, and saved the shipwrecked crew. He was called Leif the Lucky.

Leif reached land in Eiriksfjordr, and proceeded home to Brattahlid. The people received him gladly. He soon after preached Christianity and catholic truth throughout the land, making known to the people the message of King Olaf Tryggvason, and declaring how many renowned deeds and what great glory accompanied this faith.

Leif's father, Eirik, however, took coldly to the proposal to forsake his old religion, even as his wife, Thjodhild, promptly yielded and ordered a church to be built near the houses she called Thjodhild's Church. In that spot she offered her prayers, as did all those men, and they were many, who received Christ. After she accepted the faith, Thjodhild would have no sexual intercourse with Eirik, and this was a great trial to his temper.

After this there was much talk about making ready to go to the land which Leif had discovered. Thorstein, Eirik's son, was chief mover in this, a worthy man, wise and much liked. Eirik was also asked to go, and they believed that his luck and foresight would be of the highest use. He was [against it, but did not say no], when his friends exhorted him to go. They made ready the ship which Thorbjorn had brought there, and there were twenty men who undertook to start in her. They had little property, chiefly weapons and food. On the morning when Eirik left home he took a little box which had in it gold and silver and he hid the money then went forth on his journey.

However, he had proceeded but a little way when he fell from his horse and broke his ribs and injured his shoulder, and cried out, *"Aiai!"* He sent word about this accident to his wife, telling her she should take away the money that he had hidden, declaring his misfortune to be a penalty paid on account of having hid the money. Afterwards Thorstein sailed away out of Eiriksfjordr with gladness, as their plan seemed to promise success.

They were driven about for a long time on the open sea, not coming onto the track which they desired. They came in sight of Iceland and also met with birds from the coast of Ireland. Then their ship was tossed to and fro on the sea. They returned about harvest-tide, worn out and much exhausted by toil, reaching Eiriksfjordr at the beginning of winter.

Then spoke Eirik, *"You were in better spirits in the summer, when you went forth out of the fjord, than you are in now, and yet for all that there is much to be thankful for."*

Thorstein replied, *"It is a chieftain's duty now to look after some arrangement for these men who are without shelter, and to find them food."*

"That is an ever-true saying, 'You know not until you have got your answer.'" Eirik replied. *"I will now take your counsel about this."*

All those who had no other abodes, were to go with the father and the son. Then they came to land, and went forth home.

Chapter 6

Now, after this, I have to tell you how Thorstein, Eirik's son, began wooing Gudrid, Thorbjorn's daughter. A favorable answer was given to his proposals, both by the maid herself and by her father. Also, the marriage was arranged so that Thorstein would take possession of his bride at Brattahlid when the bridal feast was held there in the autumn. The banquet went off well and was attended by many.

Thorstein owned a homestead in the Vestribygd on the estate known as Lysufjordr (Shining fjord). A man who was called "Thorstein the Black" owned the other half of the homestead. His wife was called Sigrid. That autumn both Thorstein and Gudrid went to his namesake at Lysufjordr. Their reception was a welcome one.

They spent the winter at Lysufjordr when fever broke out on their estate. The overseer of the work was named Garth. An unpopular man, he took the fever first and died. Afterwards, and with but little intermission, one after another took the fever and died. Then Thorstein, Eirik's son, fell ill, and also Sigrid, the wife of his namesake "Thorstein the Black".

And one evening Sigrid left the house and rested awhile opposite the outer door when Gudrid accompanied her.

"We have come outside without thinking." Gudrid said, feeling the chill of the night air. *"And there is no way you can withstand this cold! Let us go home as quickly as possible."*

Sigrid looked back towards the outer door and she had a vision then screamed out aloud. *"It is not safe as matters are!"* she said. *"There is all that crowd of dead people before the door!"* Thorstein, Eirik's son, was in her the vision. He seemed to have had a whip in his hand, wishing to smite the ghostly troop. *"I also recognized Thorstein, your husband, and myself among them! And it is a grief thus to behold!"*

Then the vision faded away. *"Gudrid!"* she said, *"Let us go now! I see the crowd no longer."*

And they went inside; but before morning came, Sigrid was dead, and a coffin was prepared for the body.

Now, that same day, the men purposed to go out fishing and "Thorstein the Black" led them to the best fishing places. In the early morning he went to see what they had caught. Then Thorstein, Eirik's son, sent word to his namesake to come back quickly, saying that matters at home were hardly quiet. Gudrid was endeavoring to rise to her feet and to get under the blankets beside him; and when he came in she had risen upon the edge of the bed. Then he took her by the hands and laid a pole-axe upon her breast. Thorstein, Eirik's son, died near nightfall. Thorstein, the franklin, begged Gudrid to lie down and sleep, saying that he would watch over the body during the night, so she did. The night was little of past when Thorstein, Eirik's son, suddenly sat up and spoke, saying he wished Gudrid to be called to him, and that he wished to speak with her.

"God wills that this last hour be given to me for my own," he said, *"and the further completion of my plan."* Thorstein, the franklin, went to find Gudrid, and woke her. He first begged her to cross herself and to ask God for help; then told her what Thorstein, Eirik's son, had said to him; *"And he wishes to meet with you."* He said. *"You are obliged to consider what plan you will adopt, because I can in no way advise you on this issue."*

She answered, *"It may be that this - this wonderful thing - has regard to certain matters which are afterwards best left in memory. I hope that by keeping God it will test upon me, and I will, with God's grace, undertake the risk and go to him and hear what he has to say, for I shall not be able to escape if harm must happen to me. I am far from wishing that he should go elsewhere; I suspect, moreover, that the matter will be a pressing one."*

Then Gudrid went and saw Thorstein. He appeared to her as if shedding tears. He spoke in a low voice in her ear, whispering certain words which she alone might know. But this he said so that all could hear: *"Those men who hold the true faith will be blessed. And although salvation and mercy accompanies it, many, nevertheless, hold it lightly."*

"It is not a good custom which has prevailed here in Greenland since Christianity came; to bury men in unconsecrated ground with but few religious rites said over them. I wish for myself, and for those other men who have died, to be taken to the church.

"But for Garth, I wish him to be burned on a funeral pile as soon as may be! For **he** *is the cause of all those ghosts which have been among us this winter!"*

Thorstein also spoke to Gudrid about her own state, saying that her destiny would be a great one and begged her to beware of marrying Greenland men. He begged her also to pay over their property to the Church and some to the poor. Then he sank down for the second time, lifeless.

It had been a custom in Greenland, after Christianity was brought there, to bury men in unconsecrated ground on the farms where they died. An upright stake was placed over a body, and when the priests came to the place afterwards, the stake was then pulled out, consecrated water poured therein, and a funeral service held, though it might be long after the burial.

The bodies were removed to the church in Eiriksfjordr and funeral services held by the priests. After that Gudrid's father, Thorbjorn, died and the whole of his property also went to Gudrid. Eirik received her into his household, and looked after her stores well.

Chapter 7

In the north of Iceland, at Reynines in Skagafjordr, as it is now called, there dwelt a man named Thorfinn Karlsefni, son of Thord Horsehead. Karlsefni was a man of good family, and very rich. His mother's name was Thorun. He engaged in trading journeys and seemed a goodly, bold, and gallant traveler.

One summer Karlsefni prepared his ship, intending to go to Greenland. Snorri, Thorbrand's son, from Alptafjordr, resolved to travel with him. There were thirty men in the company.

The very same summer as Karlsefni, there was a man named Bjarni, Grimolf's son, a man of Breidafjordr (Broadfirth); and another man from the east of Iceland called Thorhall, son of Gamli, who also prepared their ship with the intent to go to Greenland. In the ship they had forty men total. The two ships launched out into the open sea as soon as they were ready. It is not recorded how long a voyage they had.

But, after this, I have to tell you that both these ships came to Eiriksfjordr about autumn. Eirik rode down to the ships with other men of the land, and a market-fair was promptly instituted. The captains invited Gudrid to take such of the merchandise as she wished. On his part, Eirik displayed much magnificence in return, inasmuch as he invited both these ships' companies' home with him to pass the winter in Brattahlid. The merchants accepted the invitation, and went home with Eirik. Afterwards their merchandise was removed to Brattahlid, where there was a good and large outbuilding in which to store the goods. The merchants were well pleased to stay with Eirik during the winter.

When now Yule was drawing near, Eirik began to look gloomier than usual. Presently Karlsefni entered into conversation with him, and said, *"Are you in trouble, Eirik? It appears to me that you are somewhat more taciturn than you have been. Still, you help us with much liberality and, as we have means, we are bound to reward you accordingly. Tell me what causes your gloominess."*

"You receive hospitality well and like worthy men, now." Eirik answered, *"I have no desire that our dealings together should be expensive to you. But to me it will seem a terrible thing if it is heard that you never spent a worse Yule than when Eirik the Red entertained you at this one, just now beginning, at Brattahlid, in Greenland."*

Karlsefni answered, *"Such must not come to a pass. We have in our ships malt, meal, and corn and you have right and title to take from there whatever you wish and to make your entertainment such as agrees with your generosity."*

And Eirik accepted the offer. Then preparation was made for the Yule-feast. So magnificent it was that the men thought they had scarcely ever seen so grand a feast.

After Yule, Karlsefni came to Eirik and broached the subject of a marriage with Gudrid. The woman appeared to him to be both beautiful and of excellent understanding and he thought, might be under Eirik's control.

"For my part I will willingly undertake your suit." Eirik answered. *"She is worthy of a good match. She will be following her destiny should she be given to you. Moreover, the report of you which comes to me is good."*

The proposals were now laid out before her, and she allowed the marriage with her to be arranged which Eirik wished to promote. However, I will not now speak at length how this marriage took place.

The Yule festival was prolonged and made into a marriage-feast and there was great joy in Brattahlid during that winter. Much backgammon playing and telling of stories went on, and many things were done that ministered to the comfort of the household

Chapter 8

During this time much talk took place in Brattahlid about making ready to go to "Vinland the Good" and it was asserted that they would find there good choice lands. The discourse came to such conclusion that Karlsefni and Snorri prepared their Knorr with the intention of seeking Vinland during the summer, with Bjarni and Thorhall venturing on the same expedition, with their ship and the retinue which had accompanied them, including Thorvard, husband of Freydis, the natural daughter of Eirik the Red;, as also did Thorvald, a son of Eirik.

Thorhall was Eirik the Red's son-in-law and was called the Sportsman; for he had been Eirik's companion in hunting and fishing expeditions for a long time, and during the summers many things had been committed to his keeping.

Thorhall was a big man, silent at all times, gaunt and dark in appearance; and rather advanced in years. Overbearing in temper and of melancholy mood, he was underhanded in his dealings, given to abuse and always inclined towards the worst. He had kept himself aloof from the true faith when it came to Greenland. He was but little encompassed with the love of friends, but yet Eirik had long held conversation with him.

Now, when Leif was with King Olaf Tryggvason, and the king had requested him to preach Christianity in Greenland, he gave him two Scottish people, a man called Haki and a woman called Hækja. The king requested that Leif use these people if ever he should want fleetness because they were swifter than the wild beasts. Eirik and Leif had Haki and Hækja go with Karlsefni.

Thorhall went in the ship with Thorvald and his men, because he was widely acquainted with the unpeopled districts. They had the ship which Thorbjorn had brought to Greenland and they ventured on the same expedition with Karlsefni and Bjarni; most of them in this ship being Greenlanders. There were one hundred and sixty men total in the ships.

They sailed away from land then to the Vestribygd; from there to the Bjarneyjar (Bear Islands). Then they sailed away from Bjarneyjar on northerly winds and were out at sea for two and a half days before they came to land. They rowed along the coastline in boats and explored there, finding flat stones, so many and great that two men might well lie on them stretched on their backs with heel to heel. Polar-foxes were there in abundance. This land they gave name to and called it Helluland (stone-land).

Then they sailed with northerly winds two and a half days, and there before them was a land with a great forest and many wild beasts upon it. An island lay in the south-east off the land and they found bears thereon and called the island Bjarney (Bear Island). But the mainland, where the forest was, they called Markland (forest-land).

Then, when another two and one half days were passed, they saw land and sailed to a cape to which they came. They cruised along the land keeping it on the starboard side. There was a coast showing no natural harbors with long sandbars stretching out into the water. They went to the land in small boats and found the keel of a ship and called the place Kjalar-nes (Keelness). They gave also name to the sandbars, calling them Furdustrandir (wonder-shore), because it was tedious to sail by them. Then the coast became indented with creeks and they directed their ships along the creeks.

Now, when they had sailed past Furdustrandir, they put Haki and Hækja ashore and asked them to run into the southern regions looking for choice land, and to come back after three days had passed. Haki and Hækja were dressed in such way that they had on the garment which they called biafal. It was made with a hood at the top, open at the sides, without sleeves, and was fastened between the legs. A button and a loop held it together there; and elsewhere they were without clothing.

Then they cast the anchors from the ships and lay there to wait for them. And when three days were expired Haki and Hækja leapt down into the boat from the land. Haki had in his hand a bunch of grapes; Hækja, an ear of wild wheat. They said to Karlsefni that they believed they had found good and choice land.

Then they received them into their ship and proceeded on their journey to where the shore was cut into by a firth (fjord). They directed the ships within the firth. There was an island lying out in front of the firth, and there were great currents around the island, which they called Straums-ey (Stream-island). There were so many birds on it that scarcely was it possible to put one's feet down for the eggs. They continued their course up the firth, which they called Straumsfjordr (Stream fjord) and carried their cargo ashore from the ships, and there they prepared to stay. There were mountains and the place was fair to look upon.

They had cattle of all kinds with them; and as for themselves they sought out the produce of the land around them. They gave no heed to anything except to explore the land. They remained there during the winter, which turned out to be a hard one, because, doing no work, they hadn't prepared for it. When the fishing failed they were badly off for food and they ventured out to the island, hoping that something might be got there from fishing or from what had drifted ashore. However, there was little in that spot to be had for food. But their cattle found good sustenance for they found large pastures.

After that they called upon God praying that He would send them some little store of meat, but their prayer was not so soon granted as they were eager that it should be.

Thorhall disappeared from sight one day and they went to find him, searching continuously for three days. On the fourth day Karlsefni and Bjarni found him on the peak of a crag. He lay with his face to the sky, with both eyes and mouth and nostrils wide open, clawing and pinching himself, and reciting something. They asked why he had come there.

"It is of no importance." He replied. *"I beg of you not to worry about it. As for me, I have lived a long life and you need not take any account of me."*

They begged him to go home with them, and he did so.

A little while after this a whale was driven ashore, and the men crowded round it, and cut it up, and still they knew not what kind of whale it was. Even Karlsefni did not recognize it, though he had great knowledge of whales.

Then Thorhall stepped up and said, *"Has it not been that the Redbeard has proved a better friend than your Christ? This was my gift for the poetry which I composed about my patron, Thor; seldom has he failed me."*

It was cooked by the cook-boys, and they ate it, although all quickly became sick from it afterwards. When the other men saw what happened, none of them would eat of it, and they threw the carcass down from the rocks and turned with their supplications to God's mercy. Then was granted to them opportunity of fishing, and after that there was no lack of food that spring. They went back again from the island, within Straumsfjordr, and obtained food from both sides; from hunting on the mainland, and from gathering eggs and from fishing on the side of the sea.

Chapter 9

When summer was at hand they discussed how to proceed on their journey and made an arrangement. Thorhall the Sportsman wished to proceed northwards along Furdustrandir, and off Kjalarnes, to seek Vinland. But Karlsefni desired to proceed southwards along the land and away from the east, because the land appeared better to him the further south he went. Also, he thought it also more advisable to explore in both directions. Then did Thorhall make ready for his journey out by the islands and there volunteered for the expedition with him not more than nine men; but with Karlsefni there went the remainder of the company. And one day, when Thorhall was carrying water to his ship, he said *"The clashers of weapons did say when I came here that I should have the best of drink, though it doesn't become me to complain before the common people."*

He drank then recited this verse:

Eager God of the war-helmet!

I am made to raise the bucket;
Wine has not moistened my beard,
Rather do I kneel at the fountain.

Afterwards they put to sea, and Karlsefni accompanied them by the island. Before they hoisted sail Thorhall recited a verse:
"We go back to where our countrymen are.
Let us make the skilled hawk of the sand-heaven
Explore the broad ship-courses;
While the dauntless rousers of the sword-storm,
Who praise the land, and cook whale, dwell on Furdustrandir."
Then they left, and sailed northwards along Furdustrandir and Kjalarnes, and attempted there to sail against a wind from the west. A gale came upon them, however, and drove them onwards against Ireland, and there were they severely treated, enslaved, and beaten. Then Thorhall lost his life.

Chapter 10

However, Karlsefni with Snorri and Bjarni and the rest of the company had proceeded southwards along the land. They journeyed a long while until they arrived at a river which came down from the land and fell into a lake and so on to the sea. There were large islands off the mouth of the river but they could not come into the river except at high flood-tide.

Karlsefni and his people sailed to the mouth of the river, and called the land Hóp (Lagoon). There they found fields of wild wheat wherever there were low grounds; and the (grape) vine in all places where there was rough rising ground.

Every rivulet there was full of fish. They dug holes on the beaches where the land and water joined and the tide went highest; and when it ebbed they found halibut in the holes. There was great plenty of wild animals of every form in the wood. Having their cattle with them, they remained there half a month, amusing themselves, and not becoming aware of anything.

Early one morning, as they looked around, they beheld nine canoes made of hides, and snout-like staves were being brandished from the boats, and they made a noise like flails, and twisted round in the direction of the sun's motion.

Then Karlsefni said, "What could this be a token of?"

Snorri answered him, "Maybe it is a token of peace. Let us take a white shield and go to meet them."

And so they did. Then those in the canoes rowed forwards, and showing surprise at them, came to land. They were short men, ill-looking with large eyes and broad cheeks;

their hair in disorderly fashion on their heads. And they stayed there awhile, staring in astonishment. Afterwards they rowed away off the headland to the south.

Chapter 11

Karlsefni's men built their settlements up above the sea, some of the dwellings well inland, and some near the water, and remained there that winter. They had no snow whatever and all their cattle went out to graze without keepers.

One morning in early spring they beheld a fleet of hide-canoes off the headland rowing towards them from the south. There were so many it was as if the sea were strewn with pieces of charcoal, and there was also the brandishing of staves as before from each boat. Then Karlsefni's men held their shields up, and a market was formed between them. The people preferred red cloth in their purchases, in exchange for which they had furs to give, and skins quite grey. They wished also to buy swords and lances, but Karlsefni and Snorri forbad it. They offered for the cloth dark hides, and took in exchange a span long of cloth, and bound it round their heads; and so matters went on for a while. But when the stock of cloth began to grow small, then they split it asunder, so that it was not more than a finger's breadth. The Skrælingar (Esquimaux) gave for it still quite as much, or more than before

Chapter 12

Now it came to pass that a bull, which belonged to Karlsefni's people, rushed out of the wood and bellowed loudly at the same time. The Skrælingar, frightened thereat, rushed away to their canoes, and rowed south along the coast. There was then nothing seen of them for three weeks together. When that time was gone by, there was seen approaching from the south a great crowd of Skrælingar boats, coming down upon them like a stream, the staves this time being all brandished in the direction opposite to the sun's motion, and the Skrælingar were all howling loudly. Then Karlsefni's people picked up their red shields to meet them. They encountered one another and fought, and there was a great shower of missiles from the Skrælingar's war-slings, or catapults.

Then Karlsefni and Snorri saw that the Skrælingar were bringing up poles, each with a very large ball attached: dark in color and to be compared in size to a sheep's stomach. These flew over Karlsefni's company towards the land, and when they came down they struck the ground with a hideous noise. This produced great terror in Karlsefni and his company, so that their only impulse was to retreat up the country along the river, because it seemed as if crowds of Skrælingar were driving at them from all sides, and they didn't stop until they came to certain crags. There they offered them stern resistance.

Freydis came out and saw how they were retreating. She called out, *"Why do you run away from such worthless creatures, stout men that you are, when, as seems likely to me,*

They gave no heed to what she said.

Freydis still endeavored to accompany them, but soon lagged behind because she was with child. She followed them into the wood with the Skrælingar directing their pursuit after her. She came upon a dead man, Thorbrand, Snorri's son, with a flat stone fixed in his head, his sword on the ground beside him. She took up the sword and prepared to defend herself. Then the Skrælingar came upon her and she let down her sark and struck her naked breast with the sword. At this they were frightened, rushed off to their boats, and fled away.

Karlsefni and the rest came up to her and praised her zeal. Two of Karlsefni's men fell, along with four of the Skrælingar, notwithstanding they had overpowered them by superior numbers. After that, they proceeded to their booths (houses) and began to reflect about the crowd of men which attacked them upon the land; it appeared to them now that the one troop will have been that which came in the boats, and the other troop will have been a delusion of sight.

The Skrælingar also found a dead man, and his axe lay beside him. One of them struck a stone with it, and broke the axe. It seemed to them good for nothing, as it did not withstand the stone, and they threw it down.

Chapter 13

Karlsefni and his company were now of opinion that though the land might be choice and good, there would be always war and terror overhanging them from those who dwelt there before them. They made ready, therefore, to move away, with intent to go to their own land. They sailed forth northwards, and found five Skrælingar in jackets of skin, sleeping near the sea, and they had with them a chest, and in it was marrow of animals mixed with blood; and they considered that these must be outlaws and slew them.

Afterwards they came to a headland and a multitude of wild animals; and this headland appeared as if it might be a cake of cow-dung, because the animals passed the winter there.

Now they came to Straumsfjordr, where also they had abundance of all kinds. It is said by some that Bjarni and Freydis, and a hundred men remained there, and didn't go any further. But Karlsefni and Snorri, and forty men with them, continued to journey southwards after staying scarcely two months at Hop.

When Thorhall failed to come back the same summer, Karlsefni set out with a single ship to seek him, but the rest of the company remained behind. He and his people went northwards off Kjalarnes, and were then borne onwards towards the west, and the land lay on their larboard-side, and was nothing but wilderness. When they had proceeded for a long time, they found a river which came down from the land, flowing from the east towards the west. They directed their course within the river's mouth, and lay opposite the southern bank.

Chapter 14

One morning Karlsefni's people watched a glittering speck, as it were, above the open space in front of them and they shouted at it. It stirred itself, and it was a being from a race of men that have only one foot, and he came down quickly to where they lay. Thorvald, son of Eirik the Red, sat at the tiller, and the One-footer shot him with an arrow in the lower abdomen. He drew out the arrow. Then said Thorvald, *"Good land have we reached, and fat is it about the paunch."*

Then the One-footer leapt away again northwards. They chased after him, and saw him occasionally, but it seemed as if he would escape them. He disappeared at a certain creek. Then they turned back and one man spoke this ditty:

"Our men chased, all true it is, a One-footer down to the shore; but the wonderful man strove hard in the race.... Hearken, Karlsefni."

Then they journeyed away back again northwards, and saw, as they thought, the land of the One-footers. They wished, however, no longer to risk their company. They conjectured the mountains to be all one range; those, that is, which were at Hop, and those which they now discovered; almost answering to one another; and it was the same distance to them on both sides from Straumsfjordr. They journeyed back, and were in Straumsfjordr the third winter. Then fell the men greatly into backsliding. They who were wifeless pressed their claims at the hands of those who were married.

Snorri, Karlsefni's son, was born the first autumn, and he was three winters old when they began their journey home. Now, when they sailed from Vinland, they had a southern wind, and reached Markland, and found five Skrælingar; one was a bearded man, two were women, two children. Karlsefni's people caught the children, but the others escaped and sunk down into the earth. And they took the children with them, and taught them their speech, and they were baptized. The children called their mother Vætilldi, and their father Uvægi. They said that kings ruled over the land of the Skrælingar, one of whom was called Avalldamon, and the other Valldidida. They said also that there were no houses, and the people lived in caves or holes. They said, moreover, that there was a land on the other side over against their land, and the people there were dressed in white garments, uttered loud cries, bare long poles, and wore fringes. This was supposed to be Hvitramannaland (whiteman's land). Then came they to Greenland, and remained with Eirik the Red during the winter

Chapter 15

Bjarni, Grimolf's son, and his men were carried into the Irish Ocean, and came into a part where the sea was infested by ship-worms. They did not find it out before the ship was eaten through under them; then they debated what plan they should follow. They had a ship's boat which was smeared with tar made of seal-fat. It is said that the ship-worm will not bore into the wood which has been smeared with the seal-tar. The counsel and advice of most of the men was to ship into the boat as many men as it would hold. Now, when that was tried, the boat held not more than half the men. Then Bjarni advised that it should be decided by the casting of lots, and not by the rank of the men, which of them should go into the boat; and inasmuch as every man there wished to go into the boat, though it could not hold all of them; therefore, they accepted the plan to cast lots who should leave the ship for the boat. And the lot so fell that Bjarni, and nearly half the men with him, were chosen for the boat. So then those left the ship and went into the boat who had been chosen by lot so to do.

And when the men were come into the boat, a young man, an Icelander, who had been a fellow-traveller of Bjarni, said, "Dost thou intend, Bjarni, to separate thyself here from me." "It must needs be so now," Bjarni answered. He replied, "Because, in such case, thou didst not so promise me when I set out from Iceland with thee from the homestead of my father." Bjarni answered, "I do not, however, see here any other plan; but what plan dost thou suggest?" He replied, "I propose this plan, that we two make a change in our places, and thou come here and I will go there." Bjarni answered, "So shall it be; and this I see, that thou labourest willingly for life, and that it seems to thee a grievous thing to face death." Then they changed places. The man went into the boat, and Bjarni back into the ship; and it is said that Bjarni perished there in the Worm-sea, and they who were with him in the ship; but the boat and those who were in it went on their journey until they reached land, and told this story afterwards.

Chapter 16

The next summer Karlsefni set out for Iceland and Snorri with him, and went home to his house in Reynines. His mother considered that he had made a shabby match, and she was not at home the first winter. But when she found that Gudrid was a lady without peer, she went home, and their association was happy. The daughter of Snorri, Karlsefni's son, was Hallfrid, mother of Bishop Thorlak, the son of Runolf. (Hallfrid and Runolf) had a son, whose name was Thorbjorn; his daughter was Thorun, mother of Bishop Bjarn. Thorgeir was the name of a son of Snorri, Karlsefni's son; he was father of Yngvild, the mother of the first Bishop Brand. And here ends this story.

The Greenlanders Saga
(Grœnlendinga saga)

Chapter 1

Thorvald was a son of Osvald, a son of Ulf-Oxne-Thorersson. Thorvald and his son "Erik the Red" moved from Jæder (in Norway) to Iceland, in consequence of murder. At that time was Iceland colonized wide around. They were living at Drange on Hornstand; when Thorvald died. Erik then married Thorhild, the daughter of Jærunda and Thorbjorg Knarrarbringa (who afterwards married Thorbjorn of Haukadal).

Then Erik traveled north and lived at Erikstad near Vatshorn. Leif was the son of Erik and Thorhild. But after Eyolf Soers and "Rafn the Duelist's" murder, Erik was banished from Haukadal, and moved westwards to Breidafjord, and lived at Oexney at Erikstad. There he lent Thorgest his seat-posts, but could not get them back again. Erik then demanded them which began many disputes and frays between him and Thorgest, (as is told in Erik's saga). Styr Thorgrimson, Eyulf of Svinoe, and the sons of Brand of Alptafjord, and Thorbjorn Vifilson assisted Erik in this matter, but the sons of Thorgeller and Thorgeir of Hitardal stood by the Thorgestlingers.

Erik was declared outlawed by the Thornesthing, and he then made ready his ship in Erik's creek, and when he was ready, Styr and the others followed him out past the islands. Erik told them that he intended to go in search of the land, which Ulf Krages son Gunnbjorn saw, when he was driven out to the westward in the sea, the time when he found the rocks of Gunnbjorn. He said he would come back to his friends if he found the land.

Erik sailed out from Snæfellsjokul; he found land, and came in from the sea to the place which he called Midjokul; it is now Blaserkr. He then went southwards to see whether it was there habitable land. The first winter he was at Eriksey, nearly in the middle of the eastern settlement. The next spring Erik moved to Eriksfjord and built his farm, which he called Brattahlid, there. That summer he traveled to the western settlement and gave names to many places.

Erik spent the second winter at Holm in Hrafnsgnipa; and the third summer he took his ship and went to Iceland and landed at Breidafjord. He called the land which he had found Greenland, because, he said, *"People will be more inclined to move here if the land has a good name."*

Erik was in Iceland for the winter, but as soon as summer came, returned to Greenland to colonize the land and dwelt at Brattahlid in Eriksfjord. Informed people say that thirty-five ships joined with "Erik the Red" from Breidafjord and Borgafjord to colonize Greenland, but only fourteen arrived. Some had been driven back and others were lost at sea. This was fifteen winters before Christianity was established by law in Iceland.

"Erik the Red", who was the most respected, lived at Brattahlid, and every one regulated themselves by him. These were Erik's children: Leif, Thorvald and Thorstein, and Freydis, his (illegitimate) daughter, who was married to a man named Thorvard and they lived in Garde, where the Bishop's seat is now. She was very haughty and Thorvard narrow-minded and it was no secret she married him chiefly on account of his money. Heathen were the people in Greenland at this time.

The following men who went out with Eirik took land in Greenland: Herjulf took Herjulfsfjord (he lived at Herjulfsness), Ketil Ketilsfjord, Rafn Rafnsfjord, Sœlve Sœlvedal, Helge Thorbrandsson Alptefjord, Thorbjornglora Siglefjord, Einar Einarsfjord, Hafgrim Hafgrimsfjord and Vatnahverf, Arnlaug Arnlaugsfjord. But some went to the western settlement.

Chapter 2

Herjulf, a very respectable man, was the son of Bard Herjulfson; a kinsman to the colonist Ingolf. Herjulf was given land by Ingolf, between Vog and Reykjaness, he called Herjulfsness. Herjulf lived first at Drepstock with Thorgerd his wife, and Bjarne, their son, who was a very confident and optimistic man.

At a young age Bjarne developed a desire to travel abroad and soon earned for both riches and respect. Every second winter he spent abroad; every other at home with his father. Soon Bjarne was able to purchase his own ship. During the last winter Bjarne spent in Norway, Herjulf, meanwhile, prepared to voyage to Greenland with Erik. In the ship with Herjulf was a Christian from the Hebrides, who made a hymn respecting the whirlpool, in which was the following verse:

O thou who try holy men!
Now guide me on my way,
Lord of the earth's wide vault,
Extend your gracious hand to me!

Bjarne sailed to Eyrar with his ship the summer only to find out his father, Herjulf, had sailed away in spring. His father's actions appeared serious to Bjarne and he was now unwilling to unload his ship. When his seamen asked him what he would do, he answered: *"I intended to continue my custom and pass the winter at my father's house."* he said. *"Then I will bear for Greenland, if you will give me your company, although our voyage may appear irresponsible since none of us has been to Greenland."*

All said that they would follow his counsel. They put to sea as soon as they were ready and sailed for three days until the land behind them was under the horizon. But then the fair wind fell and there arose north winds and heavy fogs which didn't allow them to determine their position. It continued that way for many days before they saw the sun again and could discover the sky.

Now able to find their bearings, they made sail and sailed all that day before they sighted land. They counselled with each other about what land it could be and Bjarne said: *"I do not think it could be Greenland."*

They asked whether he wished to sail to this land or not.

"My advice is to sail close to the shore." he said.

And so they did, and soon saw that the land was without mountains and covered with forest, and had small heights. Then they sailed north leaving the land on their larboard (left) side, then let the stern turn from the land. Afterwards they sailed two days before they saw another land. They asked if Bjarne thought that this was Greenland, but he said: *"I don't believe this to be Greenland any more than the other land, because in Greenland are said to be very high hills of ice."*

They soon approached the land and saw that it too was a flat land covered with forest. Then the fair wind fell and the sailors became cautious, saying *"It seems to us that we should land here."* But Bjarne was unwilling to do so. They then pretended that they were in want of both wood and water.

"You have no want of either of the two." Bjarne declared, and bade them make sail. However, for this he met with some reproaches from the sailors even as it was done. They turned the prow from the land, and catching a southwest wind, sailed out into the open sea for three days before they saw the third land. Now this land was high and covered with mountains and ice-hills. Then they asked whether Bjarne would land there, but he said that he would not: *"For to me this land appears little inviting."*

He therefore did not lower the sails but instead sailed along the coast of this land, until they realized it was but an island. Again they turned the stern from the land and sailed out into the sea with the same fair wind. But as the winds grew stronger and their speed increased Bjarne ordered them to shorten the sail and not sail faster than their ship and ship's gear could hold out.

They sailed now four days before sighting the fourth land. Once again they asked Bjarne whether he thought that this was Greenland. Bjarne answered: *"This is indeed the most like Greenland, according to what I have been told about it, and it is here will we steer for land."*

So they landed in the evening under a ness, where there was a boat by the shore. Just here lived Bjarne's father, Herjulf, and from him has the ness taken its name and is since called Herjulfsness. Bjarne now repaired to his father's home and gave up seafaring. Bjarne was with his father as long as Herjulf lived, and dwelt there long after his father died.

Chapter 3

The next thing now to be related is that Bjarne Herjulfson went out from Greenland and visited Erik Jarl who received him well. Bjarne told the Jarl all about his voyages and that he had seen unknown lands. But people thought he hadn't shown enough curiosity when he had nothing to relate about these countries and this became somewhat a matter of contention to him. Bjarne became one of the Jarl's courtiers and returned to Greenland the summer after.

There was now much talk about voyages of discovery. Leif, the son of Erik the Red, of Brattahlid, went to Bjarne Herjulfson, and bought his ship from him and engaged men for it, so that there were thirty-five men in all.

Leif then asked his father Erik to be the leader on the voyage, but Erik excused himself, saying: *"I am pretty well stricken in years now and cannot, as I formerly could, withstand all the hardships of the sea."*

Leif said that Erik was still the one in the family whom good fortune would soonest attend. Erik finally gave in to Leif's request, and rode from home as soon as they were ready. Even though it was but a short way to the ship, the horse that Erik rode stumbled, and he fell off and bruised his foot. Then Erik said, *"It is not ordained that I should discover more countries than that which we now inhabit, and we should make no further attempt in company."*

Erik returned to Brattahlid, but Leif continued to the ship, his thirty-five comrades with him.

There was a southerner on the voyage, named Tyrker. Leif and his men now prepared their ship and sailed out into the sea when they were ready until they found that land first which Bjarne had seen last. There, they sailed to the land, cast anchor and put off boats, then went ashore. There was no grass, just great icebergs all over the country. A plain of flat stones extended from the sea to the mountains and it appeared to them that this land had no good qualities.

Then Leif said, *"We have not done like Bjarne about this land; we have been upon it. Now will I give the land a name, and call it Helluland."* (rocky-land)

They then returned to the ship and sailed out to sea. When they found another land they once again sailed to the land, cast anchor, then put off boats and went on shore. This land was flat, and covered with forest and the shore was low, covered with white sand beaches where ever they went. Then Leif said, *"This land shall be named after its qualities, so I name it Markland."* (wood-land)

They then immediately returned to the ship and with a northeast wind sailed out into the open sea. They were two days at sea before they saw land again and came to an island (Nantucket?) which lay to the eastward of the land. They landed in good weather and looked round them and observed that there was dew upon the grass, and it so

[83]

happened that they touched the dew with their hands, and raised the fingers to the mouth, and they thought that they had never before tasted anything so sweet.

After that they went to the ship, and sailed into a sound, which lay between the island and a ness (promontory), which ran out to the eastward of the land; and then steered westwards past the ness. The bay was very shallow at ebb tide and their ship went aground, so that the shore was far from the ship.

But so much did they desire to land, that they did not give themselves time to wait until the water again rose under their ship, but ran at once onto the shore at a place where a river flows out of a lake. As soon as the waters rose up under the ship, they then took longboats and rowed out to the ship and floated it up to the river into the lake, and there cast anchor. From the ship they brought to shore their skin cots and made their booths. After this took they counsel, making the decision of remaining there for the winter, and they built large houses there.

There was no want of salmon either in the river or in the lake, and larger salmon than they had ever seen before. The nature of the country was so good that cattle did not require house feeding in winter, for there came no frost and little did the grass wither there. Day and night were more equal than in Greenland or Iceland, for on the shortest day was the sun above the horizon from half-past seven in the forenoon till half-past four in the afternoon.

But when they had finished with the house building, Leif said to his comrades *"Now I will divide you men into two parties and have the land explored. Half of you shall remain at home at the houses, while the other half explores the land. However, travel no further than you can come home in the evening, and you should not separate."*

Now they did so for a time, and Leif had the parties switch duties, so that one day he went with them, and the other remained at home at the houses. Leif was a great and strong man, sensible and moderate in all things, grave and well favored.

Chapter 4

It happened one evening that a man of the party was missing, and this was Tyrker the German. This took Leif much to heart, for Tyrker had been long with his father and him, and loved Leif much in his childhood. Leif now took his people severely to task, and prepared to seek for Tyrker, and took twelve men with him. But when they had gotten a short way from the house, then Tyrker came towards them and was joyfully received. Leif soon saw that his foster-father was not in his right senses.

Tyrker was small and mean in stature, freckled in the face, had a high forehead and unsteady eyes, but excellent in all kinds of artifice. Then said Leif to him: *"Why are you so late? And how did you get separated from the party?"*

He spoke in German for a long time rolling his eyes about to different sides, and twisting his mouth, but they did not understand what he said. After a time he spoke

Norse. *"I have not been far off, still have I something new to tell, for I found vines and grapes."*

"Are you sure, my foster father?" Leif asked.

"I am sure," he replied, *"for I was bred up in a land where there is no want of either vines or grapes."*

They slept that night, and in the morning, Leif said to his sailors: *"We will now set about doing two things; one day we will gather grapes, and the next day cut vines and fell trees; so that from now on we will be loading the ship."*

The men agreed and it is said their long boat became filled with grapes. Now was a cargo of lumber cut down for the ship, and when the spring came they got ready and sailed away, and Leif gave the land a name after its qualities, and called it Vinland, or Wine-land.

They sailed now into the open sea, and had a fair wind until they saw Greenland, and the mountains below the joklers. Then a man put in his word and said to Leif: *"Why do you steer so close to the wind?"*

Leif answered: *"I attend to my steering but see something more, but I don't know whether it is a ship or a rock. Can't you see anything?"*

They answered that they could not observe anything out of the ordinary. Now they looked and said it was a rock. But he saw so much sharper than they that he perceived there were men upon the rock.

"Now let us hold our wind," said Leif, *"so that we come up to them. If they should want our assistance, and the necessity demands that we should help them, and if they should not be kindly disposed, the power is in our hands and not in theirs."*

Now they sailed under the rock, lowering their sails, cast anchor, and put out another little boat which they had with them. Then Tyrker called out to them *"Who is your leader?"*

"I am called Thorer," the man said *"I am a Northman; but what is your name?"*

Leif told his name.

"Are you a son of Erik the Red, of Brattahlid?" he asked.

"That is so." Leif answered. *"I will I take you all on board my ship, and as much of the goods as the ship can hold."*

They accepted this offer, and Leif rescued fifteen men from the rock and sailed from there to Eriksfjord with all the cargo except the timber, then to Brattahlid where they unloaded the ship. After that Leif invited Thorer and his wife Gudrid, and three other men to stop with him, and got berths for the other seamen, as well Thorer's, and his own, elsewhere. Leif had now earned both riches and respect and after that he was called "Leif the Lucky".

That same winter there came a heavy sickness among Thorer's people that carried off Thorer himself as well as many of his men. This same winter Erik the Red also died.

As the news spread about Leif's voyage to Vinland the excitement about exploring it grew. Thorvald, Leif's brother, thought that the land hadn't been explored enough and wanted to voyage there himself. Leif then said to Thorvald: *"You can go to Vinland with my ship, brother, if you will. But first, I wish that the ship should go and fetch the timber which Thorer had upon the rock."* and so was done.

Chapter 5

Now Thorvald made ready for this voyage with 30 men and took counsel thereon with Leif his brother. Then they made their ship ready and put to sea and nothing is told of their voyage until they came to Leif's booths in Vinland. There they laid up their ship and spent a pleasant winter and caught fish for their support.

But Thorvald said: *"In the spring we should make ready the ship and some of the men should take the ship's long boat around the western part of the land and explore there during the summer."*

To them the land appeared fair and covered with trees. A short distance between the forest, the sea and white sands, there were many islands and much shallow water. They found neither dwellings of men nor beasts, except upon an island, where to the westward they found a corn-shed of wood. But they found no other works of man and they went back and came to Leif's booths in the autumn.

But the next summer Thorvald went eastward with the ship and around the land to the northward. Here a heavy storm came upon them when off a ness so that they were driven onto shore and the keel broke off from the ship. They remained here a long time and repaired their ship. Then Thorvald said to his companions: "Now that we fixed up the keel here upon the ness, I will call it Keelness" (Kjalarness) and so they did.

After that they sailed away round the eastern shores of the land and into the mouths of the firths, which lay nearest thereto, and to a point of land which stretched out and was covered all over with wood. There, they came to with the ship and shoved out a plank to the land and Thorvald went up to the country with all his companions. He then said: "Here it is beautiful and here I would like to raise my dwelling."

Then they went to the ship and saw upon the sands within the promontory three elevations, and went thither and there saw three skin boats and three men under each. Then divided they their people, and caught them all, except one, who got away with his boat. They killed the other eight and then went back to the cape and looked round them and saw some heights inside of the fjord, and supposed that these were dwellings.

After that, so great a drowsiness came upon them that they could not keep awake and they all fell asleep. Then came a shout over them so that they all awoke. Thus said the shout: *"You, Thorvald! Wake all your companions if you wish to preserve life! Return to your ship with all your men and leave the land without delay."*

Then from the interior of the fjord rushed out an innumerable crowd of skin boats, and made towards them. Thorvald said then: *"We will put out the battle-screen and defend ourselves as well as we can, but fight little against them."* So they did, and the Skrælings shot at them for a time, but eventually ran away, each as fast as he could.

Then Thorvald asked his men if they had received any wounds; they answered: *"No; no one is wounded."*

"Good. For I have gotten a wound under the arm," he said, *"for an arrow fled between the edge of the ship and the shield, in under my arm, and here is the arrow and it will prove a mortal wound to me. Now I counsel you that you get ready to depart instantly. But you shall bear me to that cape, where I thought it best to dwell. It may be that a true word fell from my mouth, that I should dwell there for a time; there shall you bury me, and set up crosses at my head and feet, and call the place Krossaness for ever in all time to come."*

Greenland was then Christianized, but "Erik the Red" died before Christianity was the law of the land. Now Thorvald died, but they did all things according to his directions, and then went away, and returned to their companions, and told to each other the tidings which they knew, and dwelt there for the winter, and gathered grapes and vines to load the ship. But in the spring they made ready to sail to Greenland, and came with their ship in Eriksfjord, and could now tell great tidings to Leif.

Chapter 6

MEANTIME it had happened in Greenland that Thorstein in Eriksfjord married Gudrid, Thorbjorn's daughter, who had been formerly married to Thorer the Eastman, as is before related. Now Thorstein Erikson conceived a desire to go to Vinland after the body of Thorvald his brother, and he made ready the same ship, and chose great and strong men for the crew, and had with him 25 men, and Gudrid his wife.

They sailed away so soon as they were ready, and came out of sight of the land. They drove about in the sea the whole summer, and knew not where they were; and when the first week of winter was past, then landed they in Lysefjord in Greenland, in the western settlement. Thorstein sought shelter for them and procured lodging for all his crew; but he himself and his wife were without lodging, and they, therefore, remained some two nights in the ship.

Then Christianity was new in Greenland. Now it came to pass early in the morning that some people repaired to their tent and the leader of the party asked who was in the tent. Thorstein answered: *"Here are two persons. But who asks the question? Thorstein is my name."*

Said the other *"And I am called Thorstein the Black. My business here is to bid you both, you and your wife, to come and stop at my house."*

Thorstein said that he would talk the matter over with his wife, but she told him to decide, and he accepted the bidding.

"Then I will come after you in the morning with horses, for I want nothing to entertain you both. It is very wearisome at my house, for we are but two there, I and my wife, and I am very morose. I have also a different religion from yours, and yet I hold that which you have for the better."

Now he came after them in the morning with horses and they went to lodge with Thorstein the Black, who showed them great hospitality. Gudrid was a grave and dignified woman, and therefore sensible, and knew how to carry herself well among strangers.

Early that winter there came sickness among Thorstein Erikson's men, and many of his people there died. Thorstein had coffins made for the bodies of those who died, and had them taken out to the ship and laid there. *"For I will have all the bodies taken to Eriksfjord in the summer."* He said.

Now it was not long before the sickness also came into Thorstein's house and his wife, Grimhild, was the first to take sick. Grimhild was a very large woman and as strong as a man, but the sickness proved her master. Soon after that the disease attacked Thorstein Erikson and they both lay ill at the same time. Then Grimhild, the wife of "Thorstein the Black", died. And when she was dead, Thorstein went out of the room, after a plank to lay the body upon.

Then said Grimhild: *"Do not stay away long, my Thorstein!"* he answered that so it should be.

Then Thorstein Erikson said: *"How strangely is our house-mother going on. For she pushes herself up on her elbows, and stretches her feet out of bed and feels for her shoes."* At that moment the husband Thorstein came in, and Grimhild colapsed to the floor, dead, and every beam in the room creaked.

Now Thorstein made a coffin for Grimhild's body, and took it out, and buried it; but although he was a large and powerful man, it took all his strength to bring it out of the place. Now the sickness attacked Thorstein Erikson and be died, which his wife Gudrid took much to heart.

They then were all in the room. Gudrid had taken her seat upon a chair beyond the bench upon which Thorstein her husband had lain; then "Thorstein the host" took Gudrid from the chair and sat down upon another bench with her upon his knees, just opposite Thorstein's body. He comforted her in many ways, and cheered her up, and promised to go with her to Eriksfjord, with her husband's body and those of his companions.

"And I will go also," he added, *"and bring many servants to comfort and amuse you."* She thanked him.

Then Thorstein Erikson sat himself up on the bench, and said: *"Where is Gudrid?"*
Three times said he that, but she answered not.
Then said she to Thorstein the host: *"Shall I reply to him or not?"*

He counselled her not to answer. After this, "Thorstein the host" went across the floor himself and sat on a chair, and Gudrid sat upon his knees, and he said: *"What do you want, Namesake?"*

After a little while Thorstein Erikson answered: *"I strongly desire to tell Gudrid her fortune in order that she may be better reconciled to my death; for now I have come to a good resting place. But this I can tell you, Gudrid! You shall move from Greenland to Norway and from there to Iceland, where you will marry an Icelander. And you shall live long together; be very prosperous, powerful, distinguished, and excellent, sweet and well favored. You will live long and outlive him. Then you will go abroad and travel to Rome before returning again to your house in Iceland. Then a church will be built and you will reside there and become a nun, and it is there you will die."*

And when he had said these words, Thorstein fell back, dead. His corpse was set in order, and taken to the ship.

"Thorstein the host" now kept well all the promises which he had made to Gudrid; in the spring of 1006 he sold his farm, and his cattle, and with Gudrid took himself and all that he possessed to the ship then made ready and procured men for it, and then sailed to Eriksfjord. The bodies were then buried by the Church.

Thorstein the Black, who was looked upon as a very able man, made himself a dwelling at Eriksfjord and dwelt there so long as he lived.

Chapter 7

That same ship, called "Thorfinn man's material" came from Norway to Greenland. That man was Thorfinn Karlsefni by which the ship was governed. He was the son of Þórður Hesthöfði Snorrason, Þórðarson from Höfði. "Thorfinn man's material" was a Knöör and big enough to make money, and during the winter it was harbored in Brattahlid with Leif Eriksson.

And it was a good idea they had taken a break alone for Gudrid gave herself to Leif in Brattahlid. When Karlsefni found out he took a cry and tore to his ship and laid the wood on a rock for drying. Karlsefni hugged Gudrid and prayed for her, but soon it became a waste of urgency for she had succumbed to Leif's desires. She was then ordered locked in the house until she and Karlsefni were wed in the winter.

Karlsefni then asked for Leif's houses in Vinland but Leif said he would lend the houses, but not sell them. In the same meeting was a discussion, as before, on sailing to the wine country (Vinland). Karlsefni spelled out just such a journey taking both Gudrid and other men. Now his journey was planned, and he appointed a servant of six men and five women. They painted Karlsefni and his throne so that they should have all that they had for good. They had all kinds of cattle because they planned to homestead the land, if they could.

Then, in the ocean, they held a ship and came to Leifsbúður and brought up their suitcases with all the best. They soon had a great deal of good and good, because the robbery was up there, both good and good, and went on until the whale meat ran out and they lacked food. The money went up there.

After that first winter came the summer. They had all the quality of the land, which were there, both types of grapes and all kinds and quality of fish. Then they stayed at Skræling, and a great crowd of people went there out of the woods. There was near their bulls, but the graves began to call and act extensively. But Skrælingar were afraid, and buried with their burdens, and there was a gray man and a safari, and all kinds of linen, and turned to Karlsefjörður's farm, and wished to enter the houses, but Karlsefni guarded the door. Hvérigir understand another matter.

Then Skrælingar took over his lap, and let go of them, and bid them, and wished for a weapon, but Karlsefni forbade them to sell the weapon.

Okay, he is looking for advice in such a way that he asked women to carry out their equipment, and when they had a living, they wanted to buy that, but nothing else. Now Skræling bought that they wore their warnings in their days, but Karlsefni and his companions left their backs and leather goods. So they went away.

Now it is said that Karlsefni letrar made a ski-slope firmly about his farm and lived there. At that time Gudridur, Snorri's wife, gave birth to a boy child, and Karlsefni's wife named him Snorri's Lad. In the second winter, Skrælingar came to meet them and there were much more than before and had such a defense as before.

Then Karlsefni said to women, *"Now you have to carry out such food as before, but nothing else."*

Ok when they saw them, they threw their bows over the ski slope. But Gudrid sat in the durum with Snorri's son's cradle. Then there was a shadow in the doorway, and a woman in a black curtain came down, low in her head, and had a headlamp and a lightning on hair, a feeble and a lot of self-esteem, so that no eyes were seen in one man's head.

She went there when Gudríður sat, and said, "What is your name?" she says.

"My name is Gudríður, or what's your name?"

"My name is Gudríður," she says.

Then Gudríður Husfrey held her hand out to her, so that she sat by her, but it was then that Gudríðr heard a great noise, and the woman was gone, and that was the way one of the Skræling one Karlsefni's housewife, because he had wished to take their weapons, and now departed most of the time, but their clothes lay there and forever. No man had Gudríður out of this sight or left the wife alone.

"Now we will have to take it," says Karlsefni, *"for I think that they will visit us for the third time, in multitudes and for war. Now let's assume that ten men go down this nest and sample; see, there is another team going to the woods and chopping there for a bull. And when there is a rush from the forest, let's take care of us and let him go for us."*

But there was such a way that their meeting was supposed to be on water on the other side, but the other way round. Now that advice was made by Karlsefni.

The Skrælingar came to the place Karlsefni had planned for battle and there was a fight and a multitude of Skræling teams fell. One Skræling was a great and good man, and Karlsefni thought he would be their chief.

Now one of Skræling had picked up an ax and looked at it for a moment, and threw it to his companion and hit him. He fell when dead. Then he caught a big man at the ax and looked for a while, then threw her to the sea, the longest of whom he could. But then they flee to the woods, so whoever could go, and now they are trading.

Were they Karlsefni there all winter. But to warn, Karlsefni describes that he does not want to be there longer and wants to go to Greenland. Now they make their trip, and have many qualities in the vineyard, and berries and leather goods. Now they sail.

Chapter 8

Now began people again to talk about expeditions to Vinland, for voyages thereto appeared both profitable and honorable. The same summer that Karlsefni came from Vinland, came also a ship from Norway to Greenland; this ship steered two brothers, Helgi and Finnbogi, and they remained for the winter in Greenland. These brothers were Icelanders by descent, and from Austfjord.

It is now to be told that Freydis, Erik's daughter, went from her home at Garde to the brothers Helgi and Finnbogi, and bade them that they should sail to Vinland with their vessels, and go halves with her in all the profits which might be there made. To this they agreed. She then went to her brother, Leif, and begged him to give her the houses, which he had built in Vinland; but he answered the same as before, that he would lend her the houses, but not give them to her.

So was it settled between Helgi, Finnbogi and Freydis, that each ship should have thirty fighting men and their women. But Freydis broke this agreement, and had five men more, and hid them; so that the brothers knew not of it before they came to Vinland.

Now they sailed out to sea, and as arranged, they would keep together, if possible. There was little difference and the brothers were first to land, then they cleared out their ships, and bore their goods up to the house.

Then Freydis said: *"Why do you bring your things in here?"*

"Because we believed," they said, *"that the whole agreement should stand good between us."*

"Leif lent the houses to me!" she replied, *"Not to you!"*

"When it comes to nastiness," Helgi said, *"we brothers are easily excelled by you!"*

Now they took out their goods, and made a separate building, and set that building further from the strand, on the edge of a lake, and put all around in good order; but Freydis had trees cut down for her ship's loading.

Now began winter, and the brothers proposed to set up sports, and have some amusement. So was done for a time, until evil reports and discord sprung up amongst them, and there was an end of the sports, and nobody came from the one house to the other, and so it went on for a long time during the winter.

It happened that early one morning Freydis got up from her bed and dressed herself, but took no shoes or stockings. The weather was such that much dew had fallen. She took her husband's cloak, and put it on, and then went to the door of the brothers' house. A man had gone out a little before, leaving the door half open, and she opened the door, and stood silently a little while in the opening. But Finnbogi lay inside the house and was awake, and said: *"Why are you here, Freydis?"*

"I wish that you would get up." she said, *"and come outside with me, for I want to speak with you."*

He did so and they walked to a tree that lay near the dwellings, and sat down there. *"How do you like it here?"* she asked;

"I think well of the land's fruitfulness;" he answered, *"but I think poorly of the discord that has sprung up between us, for it appears to me that there is no reason for it."*

"It is as you say," She said, *"and I agree with you; but my business here is with you; I wish to change ships with you and your brother. You have a larger ship than I do, and it is my wish to leave."*

"If that is your wish," he said, *"I can agree to that."*

With that they separated, Freydis to her home and Finnbogi to his bed. She got into the bed with cold feet which immediately woke Thorvard and he asked why she was so cold and wet.

"I went to the brothers," She answered with much vehemence, *"to make a bargain with them about their ship, for I wanted to buy it because it is larger. But they took it so badly that they beat me and used me shamefully! But you! You miserable man! You neither avenge my disgrace nor your own! It is obvious that I am no longer in Greenland! I will separate from you if you don't avenge this!"*

When he could no longer withstand her reproaches he ordered his men to get up with all speed and take their arms; and so they did. They went straightway to the brothers' house and fell upon the sleeping men. They bound them and led outside one after the other, and Freydis ordered each of them killed as he came out.

Now that all the men there were killed only four women remained. But no one would kill them. Then Freydis said: *"Give me an axe!"*

So it was done; and she attacked the five women that were there and did not stop until they were all dead. Now they went back to their house after this evil work, and Freydis did not appear bothered by it at all, and spoke to her people: *"If we make it back to Greenland,"* she said, *"I will take the life of any man who tells of this business. We will say only that they remained behind when we went away."*

Now early in the spring they made ready the ship that had belonged to the brothers and loaded it with all the best things they could get, and the ship could carry. After that they put to sea, and had a quick voyage, coming to Eriksfjord with the ship early in the summer. Now Karlsefni was there, and had his ship quite ready for sea, and waited for a fair wind; and it is generally said, that no richer ship has ever gone from Greenland than that which he steered.

Chapter 9

Freydis now repaired to her dwelling which, in the meantime, had stood uninjured. She gave her companions great gifts so that they would conceal her misdeeds and now sat down in her house. However, all were not so mindful of their promises to conceal their crimes and wickedness and it came out at last.

Now it finally reached the ears of her brother Leif, and he thought very ill of the business. Then Leif took three of Freydis' men and tortured them until they confessed the whole occurrence and all their statements agreed.

"I cannot," Leif said, *"do to Freydis, my sister, that which she deserves. But this I will predict, that her posterity will never thrive."*

Now the consequence was, that no one, from that time thought otherwise than ill of Freydis and Thorvard..

Now must we begin from the time when Karlsefni got ready his ship, and put to sea; he had a prosperous voyage, and came safe and sound to Norway, and remained there for the winter and sold his goods, and both he and his wife were held in great honor by the most respectable men in Norway.

But the spring after, he fitted out his ship for Iceland; and when he was ready, and his ship lay at the bridge waiting for a fair wind, then came there a southern man to him, who was from Bremen in Saxony, and wanted to buy from Karlsefni his house broom. *"I will not sell it,"* he said.

"I will give you a gold half-mark for it," said the German.

Karlsefni thought this was a good offer, and they closed the bargain and the southern man went off with the house broom. But Karlsefni didn't know what wood it was made of; it was mausur, (birds-eye maple?) brought from Vinland.

Now Karlsefni put to sea, and came with his ship to Skagafjord, on the northern coast, and there was the ship laid up for the winter. That spring he bought Glaumbæland, and fixed his dwelling there, and lived there, and was a highly respected man. From he and Gudrid, his wife, has sprung a numerous and distinguished race. When Karlsefni died, Gudrid took over the management of the house with her son Snorri, who was born in Vinland.

And when Snorri Karlsefnesson was married, Gudrid, just as Thorstein Erikson predicted, then went abroad, and travelled southwards, to Italy, then came back again to the house of Snorri. Snorri then ordered a church to be built at Glaumbæ. After this Gudrid became a nun and recluse, and remained so the rest of her life.

Snorri had a son named Thorgeir; he was father to Ingveld, mother of Bishop Brand. The daughter of Snorri, Hallfrid, was mother to Runolf, father to Bishop Thorlak.

Bjorn, another son of Karlsefni and Gudrid, was father to Thorunn, mother of Bishop Bjarn. A numerous race is descended from Karlsefni, all distinguished men; and Karlsefni has accurately related to all men the occurrences on all these voyages, of which somewhat is now recited here.

THE PAUL KNUTSON LETTER

The following is the letter of command from King Magnus given to Paul Knutson, at Anarm, to sail to Greenland:

Magnus; by the Grace of God, King of Norway, Sweden, and Skåne, sends to all men who see or hear this letter good health and happiness in God. We desire to make known to you that you are to take all the men who shall go in the Knöörr whether thy be named or not named, from my bodyguard or other men's attendants or of other men whom you may induce to go with you, and that Paul Knutsson, who is to be commandant on the Knöörr, shall have full authority to name the men whom he thinks are best, both as officers and men.

We ask that you accept this, our command, with a right good will for the cause, as we do it for the honor of God and for the sake of our soul and our predecessors, who have introduced Christianity in Greenland and maintained it to this day, and we will not let it perish in our days. Let it be known that whoever breaks this our command shall feel our displeasure and pay us in full for the offense.

Executed in Bergen on the Monday after the Feast Day of Simon and Jude in the 36th year of our rule. Herr Orm Eysteinsson, our Lord High Constable, set the seal.